Palgrave Studies in the History of Finance

The study of the history of financial institutions, markets, instruments and concepts is vital if we are to understand the role played by finance today. At the same time, the methodologies developed by finance academics can provide a new perspective for historical studies. Palgrave Studies in the History of Finance is a multi-disciplinary effort to emphasise the role played by finance in the past, and what lessons historical experiences have for us. It presents original research, in both authored monographs and edited collections, from historians, finance academics and economists, as well as financial practitioners.

More information about this series at
http://www.palgrave.com/gp/series/14583

Mats Larsson · Kristina Lilja · Tom Petersson

Risk Management in Early Banking

An International Perspective of Swedish Savings Banks, 1820–1910

palgrave
macmillan

Mats Larsson
Department of Economic History
Uppsala University
Uppsala, Sweden

Kristina Lilja
Department of Economic History
Uppsala University
Uppsala, Sweden

Tom Petersson
Department of Economic History
Uppsala University
Uppsala, Sweden

ISSN 2662-5164 ISSN 2662-5172 (electronic)
Palgrave Studies in the History of Finance
ISBN 978-3-030-80774-0 ISBN 978-3-030-80775-7 (eBook)
https://doi.org/10.1007/978-3-030-80775-7

Cover illustration: Scottish Viewpoint/Alamy Stock Photo

This Palgrave Macmillan imprint is published by the registered company Springer Nature Switzerland AG
The registered company address is: Gewerbestrasse 11, 6330 Cham, Switzerland

Preface and Acknowledgements

The establishment of savings banks was an essential part of the development of modern banking—especially in Sweden. In this book we focus on the role of Swedish saving banks in the nineteenth century and early twentieth century, in a European perspective. This analysis covers a period when banking developed as a well-functioning system for deposits and credits. The book focuses on this development from a theoretical perspective connected to risk management and the role of trust and legitimacy in credits and savings. We analyse the role of insider lending and the practical aspects of granting credit, such as the use of collaterals and the level of interest rates to compensate higher risks. Research on savings banks has for many years been an important research field at the Department of Economic History, Uppsala University and has resulted in six Ph.D. theses and several other publications.

We want to thank the financiers of this research: HERA (Humanities in the European Research Area) for financing the UPIER project (Uses of the past in International Economic Relations) and the Sparbankernas Forskningsstiftelse (Savings Banks Research Foundation) and Enrique Rodriguez. Our sincere thanks also go to our present and previous research colleagues: Professor Håkan Lindgren and the members of the Uppsala Savings Banks research project Lars Fälting, Hilda Hellgren, Mikael Karlsson and Anders Sjölander for fruitful discussions. We are also grateful to the anonymous readers from Palgrave Macmillan for insightful comments. In the end, as always, any remaining errors are our own.

The project UPIER is financially supported by the HERA Joint Research Programme 3 Uses of the Past which is co-funded by AHRC, AKA, BMBF via DLR-PT, CAS, CNR, DASTI, ETAg, FWF, F.R.S.—FNRS, FWO, FCT, FNR, HAZU, IRC, LMT, MIZS, MINECO, NWO, NCN, RANNÍS, RCN, SNF, VIAA ant The European Commission through Horizon 2020.

HERA
Humanities in the European Research Area

This project has received funding from the Europe Union's Horizon 2020 research and innovation programme under grant agreement No. 649307.

Uppsala, Sweden

Mats Larsson
Kristina Lilja
Tom Petersson

Contents

List of Figures

List of Tables

CHAPTER 1

Introduction

Abstract Research problem and aim of the study is presented. Theoretical approach presenting the problems of legitimacy, trust and risk on financial markets. The role of personal trustworthiness, networks and regulations to create legitimacy is discussed. The structure of the study is presented.

Keywords Theory · Legitimacy · Trust · Trustworthiness · Regulations

Problem and Aims of the Study

Creating legitimacy and trust between individuals and organizations is one of the most important challenges for the development of financial systems. Uncertainty exists to a large extent due to information asymmetries but can also be connected to the uncertainty about what might happen over time. Legitimacy serves to reduce such uncertainty as well as the transaction costs. Legitimacy in the financial system is closely related to the general acceptance of both the system as such and the organizations within the system. Trust on the other hand is more personal and originates from relationships between actors on the market, created for instance through personal networks or repeated transactions

M. Larsson et al., *Risk Management in Early Banking*, Palgrave Studies in the History of Finance,
https://doi.org/10.1007/978-3-030-80775-7_1

between actors. However, trust and legitimacy are often combined and is a necessary fundament for the long-term stability of a financial system.[1]

Risk is a critical factor to be considered for depositors as well as lenders when conducting transactions. Trust between persons can reduce risks. But this also includes a well-known contradiction. Financial institutions can mediate financial risks, which at the same time makes them vulnerable to decreased trust or legitimacy.[2] This may lead to for example bank runs, crises in liquidity and financial panic. Hence, financial systems that depend on specialized financial institutions are often susceptible to periods of illiquidity or financial stress when trust in these institutions drops.

The failure of organizations specializing in financial intermediation—for example savings banks and commercial banks—may spread to other actors on the market and ultimately threaten the entire financial system. It is for this reason that we often understand financial liquidity as a public good, providing a motive for on-going government intervention, such as lender of last resort facilities. The question of legitimacy becomes even more crucial when financial systems are undergoing rapid change or when new and innovative financial systems are being established, as in Sweden during the nineteenth century.[3]

Legitimacy of and trust in financial actors were of the greatest importance during the establishment of the "modern" Swedish financial market in the 1820s. Legitimacy was the basis for the recruitment of depositors and borrowers as well as fundamental for risk management and the establishment of a banks' business activities.[4] Legitimacy was probably more important for savers than for the borrowers, but for the latter group trustworthiness was also important. Thus, it was of primary interest that a borrower could be confident that the terms of the credit were not to be changed and that the lender would not utilize information in an improper way.[5] The problems connected with banking in the nineteenth century

[1] The problems of risk, legitimacy and trust in the financial system especially in Sweden, has also been discussed—among others—by Larsson and Ögren (2019) and Gebert-Persson (2006).

[2] Diamond and Rajan (2001) and Powell and DiMaggio (1991).

[3] Larsson and Ögren (2019).

[4] See for example Gasslander (1956) and Hildebrand (1971).

[5] Hellgren (2003) and Perlinge (2005).

were thus more or less the same as today. Consequently, historical knowledge can help us understand also current risk management problems in banking.

In this book, we aim to identify and analyse risks in early banking—1820–1910—and how these risks were handled by savings banks and how risk reduction helped increasing trust and legitimacy.[6] What role did trust, and legitimacy play for the development of banking and the recruitment of costumers? How were risks handled in banks and especially how were high risks managed? Which evaluations lay behind the bank's choice of risk management?

The analysis is based on the development of Swedish savings banks between 1820 and 1910. As the novel component of the modernized Swedish financial system, savings banks are well suited as an example. Already from the 1820s savings banks were established in small towns and some rural areas. Commercial banks were founded in the 1830s, and slowly started to develop their business in larger urban areas. Savings banks played an important role in the development of the financial system, especially through their interest in small deposits from ordinary people, and at the same time lending to both private persons and small-scale industries.

The development of Swedish savings banks is an interesting example of the establishment and early development of actors in a newly launched financial system. It establishes jointly with the industrialization of Sweden and the "modernization" of the national economy and political system—as was the case in several other European countries during this period. Thus, research based on primarily the internal records from Swedish savings banks, not only gives us an insight in the development of the Swedish financial system but also presents a general picture of the relationship between banks and their customers and the role of risk, trust, and legitimacy in the development of a financial system.

[6] Research on savings banks have been carried out at the Economic History Department at Uppsala University for more than two decades. Among other publications this has resulted in six Ph.D. thesis: Fälting (2001), Petersson (2001), Sjölander (2003), Hellgren (2003), Lilja (2004) and Karlsson (2012), which all are important for the foundation and layout of this publication.

Risk, Legitimacy and Trust

A developing economy needs a financial system for both a well-functioning payment system and the transfer of financial resources. A well-functioning system includes the reduction of risks connected with transactions. Thus, the rule of legislation, traditions and norms are fundamental for the function of the financial system. Through these institutions goals of the financial system can be formalized, which govern the actors' business. In a financial system based on traditions and norms on the other hand, restrictions on business are often less detailed and the actors' activities are often not openly monitored. The difference between these two financial systems is not clear-cut. The formal financial system based on legislation and other regulatory measurements, often also include traditions, while informal systems based on traditions and norms also include some law regulations. Thus, the formal and informal financial systems often coexist in all economies.

Trust is important for all transactions on the financial market. In a credit transaction, banks must believe in the borrowers' ability to fulfil their amortization and interest payments, both in the short and long run. At the same time, the depositors must have trust in the banks' economic stability and willingness to avoid unnecessary risks that could endanger the savers deposits. The mutual trust between actors on the financial market is a necessary complement to regulations and traditions. Trust can be earned through repeated business transactions but also through direct personal contacts between the business parties.[7]

As opposed to trust, legitimacy is normally created by an external impersonal process. But legitimacy could also be created through contacts between companies or private persons who themselves have a high degree of trustworthiness. During the nineteenth century people from the business, administrative and political elite often acted as trendsetters for local and regional markets as well as on a national level. For example, when the Wallenberg-owned *Stockholms Enskilda Bank* encountered economic problems in 1878–1879 the king Oscar II personally visited the bank's office and deposited a considerable sum, in order to—with his good name—counteract the risks for a bank run.[8]

[7] Larsson and Ögren (2019).

[8] *Stockholms Enskilda Bank* (1906), Olsson (1997). The Wallenberg family was already during the late nineteenth century one of the most important business families in Sweden.

This can be regarded as an example of an unusual lender of last resort activity, but it also illustrates how individuals could promote legitimacy not only for a specific bank but also for the total financial system. However, it was more common that trustworthy persons from the local society deposited capital or in other ways wanted to promote the establishment or development of a bank.

The role of local elites has especially been highlighted by Mikael Karlsson in his study of the local elite society DBW and the establishment of the local savings bank in the town of Visby 1830.[9] The society DBW was originally established by the administrative and economic elite of Visby to arrange feasts for the members, but gradually their interest for philanthropy increased and in 1830 DBW opened a savings bank to promote savings among the poor, so that they would not need to be supported by the local community. Both the promoters and the board members of the savings bank upheld important positions in Visby—among others the mayor, the governor and the deputy chief constable—which increased the mental security for the depositors in the new bank. Many of the depositors were also recruited among workers both from the town and from the surrounding rural areas.[10]

Contacts with the informal market were also important in increasing the legitimacy of local banking business. For example, private persons with positions as lenders on informal credit markets were often regarded as trustworthy, and if they could be engaged in bank activities, they could help attract new customers. Another way of increasing bank legitimacy on the local market was to utilize the same systems for lending as for informal credit networks. This could perhaps explain why lending against personal guarantees was so important for several savings banks' businesses in the nineteenth century.

Hilda Hellgren gives us an explicit example of the importance of personal guarantees in the establishment and development of the town savings bank of Sala. Already from the start of this savings bank most lending was based on personal guarantees as collateral. With two or three guarantors for each loan and hundreds of loans, a complicated and comprehensive network of financial contacts was established. A guarantor

[9] DBW is short for *De badande Wännerna*, which translated stands for: the bathing friends.

[10] Karlsson (2012).

could have as much as between 15 and 20 commitments, which made the banks network both impervious and sensitive for economic changes. However, the average commitment was not that impressive. In 1890 there were 1050 guarantors, with a total of 2023 commitments (average 1.9 per person). But a failure of a couple of borrowers could have direct effects on the entire local financial system. This collateral system was an image of the system used on the local informal financial market where capitalists and business houses held strong positions, and where the loan scheme was built on personal trust between lenders, borrowers and guarantors.[11] The savings bank's use of this system could help to improve the trust between the banks and their customers, especially during the period when the legitimacy for the new savings banks' system was being developed.

Personal trustworthiness was used for attracting customers to banks as well as for customers to gain access to credit. Some type of relative stability and longevity in relations was a precondition for a system built on trustworthiness. In nineteenth century Sweden it was possible to build a bridge between previous trustworthy financial actors and new organizational forms. This, in turn, could also help to underpin the stability of the new and growing financial sector. Also, in nineteenth century Sweden, personal trustworthiness and networks had their limits in building and supporting legitimacy. In a growing economy with rapid changes—not least the integration of larger parts of the economy—the need for the state to support the emerging financial sector became apparent.

Molm has suggested that trust develops more easily when the exchange between two trading partners is not based on explicit negotiations and binding agreements. Instead, trustworthiness is the basis for reciprocal exchange on a market. Trust is basically dependent on the partners behaviour and position in society. The implication is that formal agreements and negotiations intended to reduce risks also might reduce trust since the incentive to develop trustworthiness was reduced.[12] Consequently, trust is more important in informal financial markets than formal markets. Trust is also strongly connected to the existence of personal networks—in fact, it is difficult to distinguish the difference between them.

[11] Hellgren (2003, pp. 142–170).

[12] Molm et al. (2000) and Larsson and Ögren (2019).

The Role of Regulation and Legislation

Legislation and other varieties of formal regulations play an important role in the establishment of banks' business, especially setting the frames for the relations between the bank and its customers. At the same time, official regulations are fundamental for the creation of legitimacy on the financial market and its actors. If we look at the establishment of the Swedish savings banks' movement, we find several examples where legislation and personal networks unite in the creation of a legitimate market.[13]

One important aspect of state regulations and activities on the financial market is to reduce risks connected with the relationship between bank and customer. This has generally been done through three different assignments; through legislation/other measurements, as inspector of the financial system and as lender of last resort. These assignments are connected to one another and activated because of changes in the market. Neither regulations nor control activities were especially developed for savings banks before 1892.[14]

During the first five decades of the Swedish savings banks' activities (1820–1875) there was no specific legislation. Instead, the savings banks' business was regulated in their charters. During the 1860s several motions were put forward in the parliament for a specific savings banks legislation to protect the depositors' capital, and in 1875 the first legislation was introduced. To avoid the mismanagement of savings banks this regulation included a compulsory reserve fund to be set aside by all banks.[15] It was obviously an attempt to increase the general trust for savings banks, but apart from this regulatory measure, not many restrictions were introduced, and savings banks' business could continue as usual.

After the acceptance of this first regulation, parliament motions were introduced to establish a special savings banks' inspectorate. It was especially the conflict of interest when the local governor was on the board

[13] See for example Karlsson (2012) and Hellgren (2003).

[14] Other state activities on the financial market are the assignment as a purchaser of financial service and as owner of a financial actor. Neither of these roles were relevant on the Swedish savings banks' market in the nineteenth century. The assignment as lender of last resort is/was not official but could be activated in the case of financial crises. See Larsson (1998).

[15] Sjölander (2003, p. 16).

of a savings bank and at the same time was responsible for the control of the bank's activities, that was regarded as a problem. However, this was not enough to persuade the parliament to introduce an inspectorate—in fact, this was not done until 1929.[16]

Instead, the most important change for the regulation of savings banks during our period of research was the introduction of the savings banks' Act 1892. It was a much more detailed regulation than the decree from 1875 and included the formalization of management as well as restriction on the banks' business.[17] Several of these regulatory measures had the purpose to harmonize the savings banks' activities, while other measures aimed to safeguard the depositors' capital. For some savings banks this legislation meant extensive changes while others could continue with business as usual.

Structure of the Study

This study consists of seven chapters, each focusing on specific problems or themes connected with early banking in Sweden generally and in the savings banks specifically. In the second chapter the overall development of the Swedish economy during the nineteenth and early twentieth centuries is presented. The focus is foremost on the transformation of Sweden from a backward economy to an industrialized and fast-growing country. The interaction between Sweden's financial sector and the growing industry laid the fundament for the fast-growing economy, but also for a general development of new financial actors.

The development of the Swedish savings banks is discussed in Chapter 3. The focus is foremost on the structural changes of the savings banks' system but also on the role of institutions in this development. The relationship between the savings banks and their customers in both depositing and lending is also highlighted.

The development of the savings banks' deposit market is in focus in Chapter 4. The role of trust is important for depositors in savings banks, but what creates this trust? Are there any differences in deposit strategy between different social groups—and if so why? What risks can be detected for depositors, and has this changed over time? We also

[16] Sjölander (2003, pp. 52–56).

[17] *SFS 1892:59*.

discuss how the banks attracted depositors and managed to keep them as customers.

Chapter 5 concentrates on the savings banks lending activities. The discussion focuses on the size of lending and its expansion during the nineteenth century. But we also analyse the use of different collaterals and changes in the composition of collaterals over time. This development can be expected to illustrate changes in the savings banks risk composition. As does also changes in the structure of borrowers.

In Chapter 6 we take the analysis of savings banks lending a bit further. Thanks to extraordinary sources in one savings bank, it is possible to reconstruct the banks risk-strategy concerning lending customers, collaterals and interest rates. We can also follow the arguments used for denial as well as acceptance of individual loans. This analysis is done on a limited benchmark period in the 1890s including the introduction of the new savings bank's legislation 1892, to see what the direct effects of the new regulatory measures were on the banks' lending.

This book ends in Chapter 7 with a concluding analysis of risk, trust and legitimacy in Swedish savings banks during the nineteenth and early twentieth centuries. The discussion is both principal and connected to specific examples from the Swedish development. Especially the rule of regulations and individual activities to generate trust and legitimacy is lifted to discussion in the establishment of savings banks.

References

Published Sources

SFS 1892:59, Lag angående sparbanker (Savings banks law).

Literature

Diamond, D. W., & Rajan, R. G. (2001), "Liquidity Risk, Liquidity Creation and Financial Fragility", *Journal of Political Economy*, Vol. 109, pp. 287–327.

Fälting, L. (2001), *Småhusfinansiering. En studie av kommunens, statens och enskilda aktörers riskhantering i Nyköping 1904–1948*. Uppsala: Acta Universitatis Upsaliensis.

Gasslander, O. (1956), *Bank och industriellt genombrott. Stockholms Enskilda Bank kring sekelskiftet 1900, del 1*. Stockholm: Generalstabens litografiska anstalt.

Gebert-Persson S. (2006), *Crash-Landing in a Turbulent Market. A Legitimating Activity*. Uppsala: Företagekonomiska institutionen.

Hellgren, H. (2003), *Fasta förbindelser. En studie av låntagare hos sparbanken och informella kreditgivare i Sala 1860–1910*. Uppsala: Acta Universitatis Upsaliensis

Hildebrand, K.-G. (1971), *I omvandlingens tjänst—Svenska Handelsbanken 1871–1955*. Stockholm: Svenska Handelsbanken.

Karlsson, M. (2012), *Filantropi under konstruktion. En undersökning av Sällskapet DBW:s samhällsengagemang 1814–1876*. Uppsala: Acta Universitatis Upsaliensis.

Larsson, M. (1998), *Staten och kapitalet—det svenska finansiella systemet under 1900-talet*. Stockholm: SNS Förlag.

Larsson, M., & Ögren, A. (2019), "Establishing Legitimacy in a New Financial System: The Central European and Baltic Experience in a Historical and Geographical Context". In M. Olsson, M. Lönnborg, & M. Rafferty (Eds.), *Unplanned: The Transformation of States and Financial Markets in "Transition" Countries*. Stockholm: Dialogos.

Lilja, K. (2004), *Marknad och hushåll. Sparande och krediter i Falun 1820–1910 utifrån ett livscykelperspektiv*. Uppsala: Acta Universitatis Upsaliensis

Molm, L. D., Takahashi, N., & Peterson, G. (2000), "Risk and Trust in Social Exchange: An Experimental Test of a Classical Proposition". *The American Journal of Sociology*, Vol. 105, pp. 1396–1427.

Olsson, U. (1997), *I utvecklingens centrum: Skandinaviska Enskilda Banken och dess föregångare 1856–1996*. Stockholm: Skandinaviska Enskilda banken.

Perlinge, A. (2005), *Sockenbankirerna. Kreditrelationer och tidig bankverksamhet. Vånga socken i Skåne 1840–1900*. Stockholm: Nordiska Museets förlag.

Petersson, T. (2001), *Framväxten av ett lokalt banksystem. Oppunda sparbank, Södermanlands enskilda bank och stationssamhället Katrineholm 1850–1916*. Uppsala: Acta Universitatis Upsaliensis

Powell, W. W., & DiMaggio, P. J. (1991) (Eds.), *The New Institutionalism in Organizational Analysis*. Chicago: The University of Chicago Press.

Sjölander, A. (2003), *Den naturliga ordningen. Makt och intressen i de svenska sparbankerna 1882–1968*. Uppsala: Acta Universitatis Upsaliensis.

Stockholms Enskilda Bank 1856–1906 (1906), Stockholm: Stockholms Enskilda Bank.

CHAPTER 2

Sweden: An Economy in Transition, 1820–1910

Abstract The transformation of society and the economic conditions in Sweden during the studied period is outlined in this chapter in a brief form. It explains how the economic growth during a period of agrarian, political and industrial revolutions increased the demand for capital as well as the need for a financial system that works efficiently and effectively.

Keywords Industrialization · Financial sector · Economic growth

When studying rapid economic transformation in the past, Sweden is, like the other Nordic countries, an interesting case. It was an industrial latecomer and had, up to the second half of the nineteenth century, a peripheral position in the European economy. From the middle of the century onward, domestic growth accelerated with the help of export-led expansion. Sawmill, iron and pulp industries were transformed as a part of technological revolution. When science, engineering and rational planning were introduced in production, a second wave of industrialization occurred in the 1890s that had new opportunities for industry and growth. From this time forward, annual GDP growths in industry and handicrafts, as well as in the transport and communication sectors, were

M. Larsson et al., *Risk Management in Early Banking*, Palgrave Studies in the History of Finance, https://doi.org/10.1007/978-3-030-80775-7_2

much higher than in the agricultural sector. Sweden quickly turned to an industrialized country before the turn of the twentieth century.[1]

The annual growth rate in Swedish GDP was higher than in the leading Western European countries and the United States during the period 1865–1910.[2] Industrial expansion did not, however, result in a radical break with the agrarian society. The early expansion was primarily driven by export-led primary produce and industrial production was mainly limited to rural areas. The agrarian revolution was, at this time, moving into a more mature stage. First, in the 1880s, industrial growth accelerated in towns, resulting in the breakthrough of an industrial society in the 1890s. At the same time, urbanization increased at a somewhat higher pace than what had occurred previously. However, still in 1910, three out of four of the circa 5.5 million inhabitants lived in the countryside. More than half of the Swedish population performed tasks in the agrarian sector. The number of inhabitants had more than doubled between 1820 and 1910, despite accelerating emigration, mainly to the United States, starting from the 1880s.[3] A growing working class and a number of important political reforms such as, for example, the introduction of the bicameral parliament in 1866 and the introduction of the modern political parties at the turn of the twentieth century, were important steps for Sweden at the beginning of the twentieth century to become a democracy.

Sweden, like other northwest European countries, deregulated its economic policy between 1850 and 1870. This free trade era had started for the domestic market during previous decades but, from the 1850s onward, more attention was paid to the relation to external markets. As a result, the Swedish economy became more integrated with the international market. Reforms such as the Companies Act of 1848, the Free Trade resolution of 1864 and the new banking legislation of 1864 were crucial for economic growth. All together, they made the foundation for the expansion of industry and trade and the modern banking sector.

[1] C. f. Schön (2012, pp. 89, 101–102, 127 and 140).

[2] Ljungberg and Schön (2013).

[3] *Historical statistics of Sweden, Part 1. Population* (1969).

Table 2.1 Average annual percentage changes of population and GDP in fixed market prices and investments in fixed prices, 1820–1910

Years	*Population*	*GDP in fixed market prices*	*GDP per capita*	*Investments in fixed prices*
1820–1830	1.1	1.7	0.6	
1830–1840	0.8	1.5	0.7	
1840–1850	1.0	2.1	1.0	
1850–1860	1.0	2.8	1.8	9.4
1860–1870	0.9	2.5	1.6	3.7
1870–1880	0.9	3.4	2.5	4.7
1880–1890	0.4	1.2	0.8	2.3
1890–1900	0.7	3.5	2.8	8.4
1900–1910	0.7	2.8	2.1	3.8

Sources *Historical statistics of Sweden Part 1. Population* (1969); Krantz and Schön (2007); Schön (2012), p. 87

The Transition Process and the Financial Sector

From the middle of the nineteenth century, infrastructure projects such as growing cities (municipal investments) and public and private investments in communication (roads, railways, telegraph, postal services and electricity from the 1880s) were significant for an economy in transformation. However, these infrastructure projects demanded many capital investments.

The Swedish economy faced a scarcity of capital for investments, as savings rates were low. Swedish households were poorer, both in per capita wealth and aggregate wealth-income ratios when compared to countries such as the United Kingdom, France and Germany. Up until World War I, the wealth-income ratio in Sweden was only half of the ratios in these leading industrial countries.[4] As a whole, GDP increased approximately six times during the period studied up to 1910. Considering GDP/capita, it increased more than three times (Table 2.1). Industrialization and emigration led to, however, rapidly increasing wages from 1880 onwards. In 1910 real wages for blue-collar workers were at approximately the same level in Sweden as in Britain.[5]

[4] Waldenström (2017, p. 310).

[5] O'Rourke and Williamson (1995, p. 179).

During the first phase of industrialization, companies mostly used their own profit for investments. The most capital-intensive projects, such as the railways for example, had to rely however on foreign capital. The import of capital had begun on a small scale for financing the transformation of the agricultural sector, but during industrialization the need for investments increased.[6] Sweden became a net importer of capital from the second half of the nineteenth century onward. During the period 1880–1910 net foreign assets were around 150 per cent of central government debt—or about the same size as the stock of the commercial bank credit. Sweden became the largest net debtor among other comparable economies.[7] It probably had the highest per capita debt of any country in 1910. Foreign debt was, however, eliminated in the beginning of the 1920s mostly because of a large trade surplus during World War I.[8]

Capital import resulted in funds being available for other projects. Sweden, like other industrialized countries, experienced a breakthrough for venture capital at the end of the nineteenth century. Collaboration between banks and the business sector was more important than it had been previously. For now on, the trade at the Stock Exchange (1863) also became more vital.[9] The growing numbers of commercials banks, insurance companies, savings banks and mortgage institutes, made up the Swedish financial market at the turn of the twentieth century. In 1897, the *Riksbank* formally became the Swedish central bank with the sole right to issue bank notes and, consequently, no longer acted as a commercial bank. After the 1870s, the improved supply of formal liquidity facilitated the possibility to allocate resources and simplified monetization. It also made everyday business easier for the many banks and other organizations that worked as intermediaries on the credit market.[10] In other words, a financial revolution was occurring in Sweden.[11]

[6] Most creditors were German and French. See Franzén (1998, p. 110).

[7] Waldenström (2017, pp. 302–303).

[8] Schön (2012, pp. 169, 171 and 175).

[9] Larsson (2016, p. 19).

[10] The supply of liquidity grew at a slow pace of an annually rate of 1.7 per cent until the late 1860s. From the 1870s the annual growth rate was much higher, 4.6 per cent. The gold standard was introduced in the 1870s. Ögren (2010, pp. 7–8).

[11] Ögren (2010).

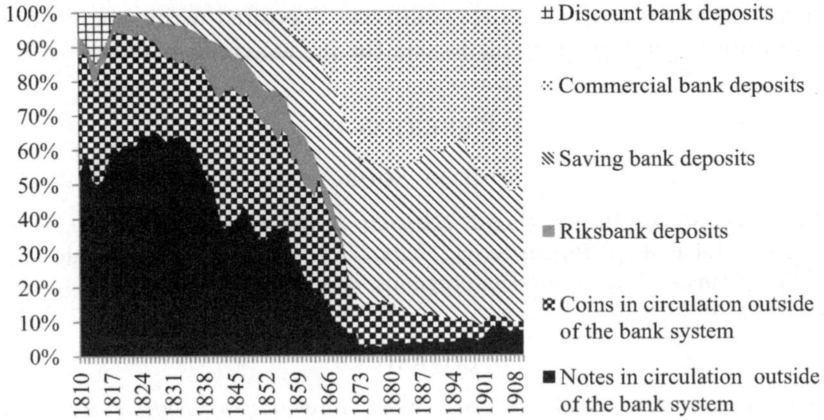

Fig. 2.1 Household bank deposits and currency, 1810–1910 (*Source* Waldenström [2021], Table SE2.3.Private sector, financial assets)

Savings banks were introduced in Sweden in the 1820s and commercial banks were given the right to run unlimited liability bank businesses and also issue notes from the bank law of 1824. The Bank Act of 1864 and the possibility of founding limited liability banks liberalized the right to establish commercial banks. Consequently, the bank sector expanded. Until the 1860s, total deposits in the financial sector grew steadily but slowly. From the middle of the 1870s until the 1890s, deposits increased with greater numbers than earlier (Fig. 2.1). However, they accelerated at an even faster pace from the 1890s onwards.[12] The financial sector grew even more as special life insurance companies were founded from the 1870s onward. During the second half of the nineteenth century, the financial institutions administered more and more of total savings, while small saver associations[13] and private capitalists administered less capital. At the turn

[12] Lilja (2010, p. 43); Fig. 3.1.

[13] The Official Financial Committee had estimated total deposits with the small savings associations located all over the country to more than 39 million SEK in 1834 and 78 million SEK in 1857. Total wealth in savings banks were the same years approximately 2 and 26 million SEK, respectively. *Underdåning betänkande angående Sveriges ekonomiska och finansiella utveckling under åren 1834–1860* (1863, pp. 71–78).

of the twentieth century, more wealth was deposited within the financial institutions than was in circulation on the private credit market.[14]

References

Online Sources

Waldenström, D. (2021), *Swedish National Wealth Database (SNWD)*, 1810–2019. Table SE2.3 *Private Sector, Financial Assets*. https://sites.google.com/view/danielwaldenstrom/data-programs. Assessed 25 March 2021.

Literature

Franzén, C. (1998), *Skuld och tanke: Svensk statsskuldsproblematik i ett internationellt perspektiv för 1930-talet*. Stockholm: Almqvist & Wicksell.

Hellgren, H. (2003), *Fasta förbindelser: En studie av låntagare hos sparbanken och informella kreditgivare i Sala 1860–1910*. Uppsala: Acta Universitatis Upsaliensis.

Historical statistics of Sweden Part 1. Population (Historisk statistik för Sverige. Del I. Befolkningen 1720–1967.) (1969), Statistics Sweden (*SCB*).

Krantz, O., & Schön, L. (2007), *Swedish Historical National Accounts 1800–2000*. Lund: Lund Studies in Economic History 41, Almqvist & Wiksell International.

Larsson, M. (2016) (Ed.), *Stockholmsbörsen på en förändrad finansmarknad*. Stockholm: SNS förlag.

Lilja, K. (2004), *Marknad och hushåll: Sparande och krediter i Falun 1820–1910 utifrån ett livscykelperspektiv*. Uppsala: Acta Universitatis Upsaliensis.

Lilja, K. (2010), "The Deposit Market Revolution". In A. Ögren (Ed.), *The Swedish Financial Revolution*. London: Palgrave Macmillan Studies in Banking and Financial Institutione, pp. 41–63.

Lindgren, H. (2002), "The Modernization of Swedish Credit Markets, 1840–1905: Evidence from Probate Records". *The Journal of Economic History*, Vol. 62, Issue 3, pp. 810–832.

Ljungberg, J., & Schön L. (2013), "Domestic Markets and International Integration: Paths to Industrialisation in the Nordic Countries". *Scandinavian Economic History Review*, Vol. 61, Issue 2, pp. 101–121.

[14] See Lindgren (2002), Hellgren (2003, pp. 61–88); Lilja (2004, c. f. p. 83), and Perlinge (2005, pp. 264–267).

Ögren, A. (2010), "The Swedish Financial Revolution: An In-Depth Study". In A. Ögren (Ed.), *The Swedish Financial Revolution*. London: Palgrave Macmillan, pp. 1–13.
O'Rourke, K. H., & Williamson, J. G. (1995), "Open Economy Forces and Late Nineteenth Century Swedish Catch-Up: A Quantitative Accounting". *Scandinavian Economic History Review*, Vol. XLIII, Issue 2, pp. 171–203.
Perlinge, A. (2005), *Sockenbankirerna: Kreditrelationer och tidig bankverksamhet. Vånga socken i Skåne 1840–1900*. Stockholm: Nordiska museets förlag.
Schön, L. (2012), *An Economic History of Modern Sweden*. London/New York: Routledge.
Underdånigt betänkande angående Sveriges ekonomiska och finansiella utveckling under åren 1834–1860. (1863), (1858 års Finanskommitté III). Stockholm.
Waldenström, D. (2017), "Wealth-Income Ratios in a Small Developing Economy: Sweden, 1810–2014". *The Journal of Economic History*, Vol. 77, Issue 1 (March 2017), pp. 285–313.

CHAPTER 3

The Savings Banks and the Swedish Banking System

Abstract The general development of the Swedish banking system and the savings banks is divided into two periods, 1820–1870 and 1870–1910. During the first phase savings banks were established with both philanthropical and economic purposes. Savings banks were crucial in developing local deposit and credit markets. During the second phase (1870–1910) the Swedish economy underwent a financial and industrial revolution. The savings banks continued to play an important role but focused their businesses more on specific segments of the local deposit and credit markets.

Keywords Banking system · Savings banks · Philanthropy · Financial revolution

During more than two centuries long existence, the savings banks in Sweden have played several different roles in developing both the financial markets and the societal economy on local, regional and national levels. The first savings banks were established in the largest towns in the 1820s and had a strong philanthropic and moralistic character, as in many other European countries. Nevertheless, from the very beginning the Swedish savings banks proved to be not merely dedicated to increasing the lower

M. Larsson et al., *Risk Management in Early Banking*, Palgrave Studies in the History of Finance,
https://doi.org/10.1007/978-3-030-80775-7_3

classes' awareness of the necessity to save and to act as morally responsible citizens. The savings banks, and their founding fathers and the first generation of managers, also had ambitions of developing the local and regional credit markets *and* to contribute to general economic growth. Hence, throughout the nineteenth and twentieth centuries the savings banks developed into one of the major players on the Swedish credit market. During the interwar period Sweden had almost 500 savings banks, which jointly had more than a 40 per cent market share on the institutional savings market. In the present day, there still are some 60 independent savings banks in Sweden, operating mainly on local and regional markets, while many of the largest savings' banks from the 1990s and on having merged into a single, nationwide bank (Swedbank) and, furthermore, changed their legal form into a public limited company, and thus became a commercial bank.

This chapter will describe the general development and the characteristics of the Swedish savings banks from the early nineteenth century up to the early twentieth century. The first chronological section, covering the years 1820–1870, deals with the first wave of establishment of savings banks, which above all took place in the larger towns. These urban savings banks were successful in their attempts to attract new layers of depositors, but nonetheless remained rather small financial organizations. The second section, covering the years 1870–1910, deals with the period of "the financial revolution" in Sweden. During this stage of development, hundreds and hundreds of savings banks were established all over the country. The savings banks managed to attract massive bulks of new customers, both depositors and borrowers, and played an important role in financing the industrial revolution in Sweden.

The Early Savings Banks, 1820–1870

The first savings bank in Sweden was established in 1820 in Gothenburg, followed by a second one in Stockholm in 1821. Another 22 savings banks were established during the rest of the 1820s and an additional 37 savings banks in the 1830s. By 1840 practically all the middle-sized or large Swedish towns had their own savings bank. During the 1850s the number of newly established savings banks rose sharply, especially in the countryside. By 1870 the total number of savings banks in Sweden was 153 (Table 3.1).

Table 3.1 The number of savings banks and commercial banks in Sweden, 1820–1870

No. of	*1820*	*1830*	*1840*	*1850*	*1860*	*1870*
Savings banks	1	25	60	85	153	251
Commercial banks[a]	0	0	-	8	30	36
Savings bank offices[b]	-	-	-	-	299	299
Commercial bank offices[b]	-	-	14	24	55	55

Source Swedish Banking Statistics, SCB
Notes [a]Commercial banks incl. 6 state-financed "branch banks" in 1855 and 19 in 1860
[b]Including head offices

In comparison to the commercial banks in Sweden, the savings banks developed much earlier and thus, as will be described later, took on the function of being market makers on numerous local credit and deposit markets. One reason for the late development of commercial banks was a combination of the strong, not to say dominant, position that the National Bank had at this point, and distrust in financial organizations on the part of the public. The Swedish financial system had gone through some harsh times in the aftermath of the Napoleonic Wars in the early nineteenth century. A handful of so-called *Diskonter* (*Discount Banks*) had been established in the late eighteenth century and the first years of the nineteenth century in the major towns outside of Stockholm, since the Parliament believed it was important that the National Bank had a monopoly in the single largest market of them all, i.e. the capital of Sweden. The Discount Banks were owned and governed either by private or public, governmental interests and offered a variety of both deposit and credit services. In 1818, however, all the Discount Banks had to close, due to a massive liquidity shortage combined with large credit losses. As a result, the public's trust in these early banks, and especially in privately owned financial organizations, was limited.[1]

Because of the breakdown of the Discount Banks, the National Bank took over as the most important institutional financial intermediator on the large regional capital markets. Furthermore, the breakdown gave private financial interests a bad reputation, which stalled the establishment of private, commercial banks for several decades. Hence, there was a

[1] Andersson (1983), Nygren (1983; 1985, pp. 29–32) and Kärrlander (2013).

window of opportunity for the savings bank at that specific time in history, not only to establish themselves as deposit institutions, but also to take on some businesses previously and traditionally performed by private financial organizations with outspoken profit interests.

A majority of the early Swedish savings banks were thus established in the towns, especially in those where official representatives of the national government were located. One characteristic of the early savings banks, and in fact the entire financial system, was thus that it was a very urban-centred system (see Table 3.2). In the establishment, governance and operation of savings banks, both private and public interests could join forces. Local elites, such as businessmen, especially within trading, large estate owners and local and regional government officials, totally dominated the early savings banks and thus gave them a second feature; one that prioritized both the philanthropic mission and at the same time the ability to develop the savings banks into long-term stable and viable financial organizations.

Philanthropy was, as for probably all European savings banks, a distinct and important explanation to the successful development of the early Swedish savings banks. In the late 1810s a government official, *Carl-David Skogman*, was given the assignment to investigate the development of the Scottish savings banks, which were considered by the government as the most successful ones at that time. Skogman's investigations were printed and then distributed in thousands of copies to local and regional government officials all over Sweden (and Finland), together with direct encouragement and recommendations aimed at the local socio-economic

Table 3.2 The geographical distribution of the Swedish savings banks, 1825–1870

Year	*In towns*		*In the countryside*		*Total*
	No.	*%*	*No.*	*%*	
1825	10	*79*	3	*21*	13
1830	22	*88*	3	*12*	25
1840	46	*77*	14	*23*	60
1850	55	*65*	30	*35*	85
1860	72	*48*	81	*52*	153
1870	82	*33*	169	*67*	251

Source Swedish Banking Statistics, SCB

elite to engage personally in the establishment of savings banks in their hometown or region. These documents were in practice transformed into normative regulations of how a savings bank was to be started and how it was to carry out its operations. The charters exemplified in Skogman's work were also copied by all new savings banks and gave the Swedish savings banks a similar and standardized form.[2]

The general philanthropic feature of savings banks in Europe at that time played an important role also in the establishment of savings banks in Sweden. The philanthropic ideas, and the savings banks' growing reputation and label as philanthropic and "good" organizations gave local elites a tenable argument to engage in the establishment and development of local savings banks. Philanthropy can be characterized as the connecting link, which made it possible to make a socio-political effort in the local community and at the same time increase one's individual wealth, prosperity and power. Besides using the savings banks to fulfil their societal duties and responsibilities as the formal and informal principals of the local communities, local elites could also get access to vital information on local money and credit markets, and in some cases, get access to capital.[3]

Deposit and Credit Market's Development

The organized, or institutionalized, banking system was in a truly embryonic development stage in the first half of the nineteenth century, despite the establishment of both savings banks and commercial banks. A large quota of the local and regional deposit and credit markets were in the hands of merchant houses, influential businesses and wealthy individuals in general. Despite this, one can characterize the savings banks as important market makers. Especially if one considers the fact that in almost all local markets a savings banks was established *before* a commercial bank or a branch office to a commercial bank. The savings banks' role as market makers was particularly important on the deposit markets. It was not until the late 1860s that total deposits in the commercial banks superseded those in the savings banks. In a Nordic comparison, however, the Swedish savings banks were not as successful as their counterparts in Denmark and

[2] Lilja (2004, pp. 50–55).

[3] Karlsson and Petersson (2006, pp. 10–12).

Norway, where the savings banks dominated the deposit markets even at the turn of the century.

From the very beginning, a clear majority of the Swedish savings banks, with the savings bank in Stockholm as the main exception, engaged heavily in lending operations, in contrast to the savings banks in Denmark, but in the same way as the savings bank in Norway. This was in fact the only investment alternative left to the early Swedish savings banks. The issuing of bonds, both private and government bonds, was at a minimal level in the first half of the nineteenth century, except for the bonds issued by the mortgage institutes. The second alternative was to try to reinvest the deposits in other, already prevalent intermediaries on the local financial markets. That would be a rather risky alternative and, in many cases, not even a conceivable alternative, simply since such willing intermediaries did not exist. It was also probably important for the newly established savings bank to offer their depositors long term and stable conditions, especially those categories that yet were not accustomed to handing over their savings to unknown financial organizations. Hence, the third alternative for the savings banks was to engage themselves in lending operations. Statistics on the investments, covering all savings banks in Sweden, are not available until the year 1850, but from this time on we know that more than 80 per cent of the deposits were transformed into loans to the public. In 1870 this quota had risen to more than 90 per cent. As a comparison, the commercial banks invested much more in bonds: between 25 and 35 per cent of their investments was placed in bonds.[4]

Turning deeper into the developments on the credit markets of the early nineteenth century, one must again point out that the informal, or unorganized, market for a long time was quantitatively speaking much larger than the institutionalized credit system. The transformation process of the credit markets, including the public's propensity to use the new financial organizations, was a slow and strenuous one. Estimations made by Håkan Lindgren and others have stated that as late as by the turn of the century 1900, credits handled by the informal sector constituted approximately 50 per cent of the total debts held by private persons.[5] The

[4] Petersson (2001, p. 75).

[5] See Lindgren (2002), Hellgren (2003, pp. 61–88); Lilja (2004, pp. 129–148) and Perlinge (2005, pp. 264–267).

Table 3.3 Advances from Swedish banks (market shares in per cent) and total volumes of advances (SEK million), 1835–1870

Year	*Savings banks, %*	*Commercial banks, %*	*The National Bank, %*	*Total volume of banking advances, SEK million*	*Total volume of the institutional credit market*[a], *SEK million*
1835	6	6	88	31	33
1840	11	21	69	46	61
1845	13	20	67	51	76
1850	18	26	56	62	99
1855	26	31	43	77	151
1860	23	44	33	121	226
1865	25	51	24	144	300
1870	26	55	19	221	415

Source Nygren (1983, pp. 29–68)
[a]Including mortgage institutes and the National Debt Office

transformation process from publicly to privately intermediated credits were, however, a rather fast one. The savings banks and the commercial banks took over as the most important lenders on the credit markets from the mid-nineteenth century and on (see Table 3.3).

Some studies have been done on the structure and characteristics of both the loans granted by the savings banks and the borrowers, respectively. The use of personal guaranteewas, not surprisingly, the dominating form of collateral in most savings banks, albeit lending against security of goods and even shares dominated in some banks, for example the savings bank in Gothenburg. Lending against real estate mortgages, finally, was not yet a distinct feature in many savings banks.[6]

The feature and characteristics of the borrowers in the early savings banks, which will be further explored in Chapter 5, was in some sense a reflection of the founding fathers of the savings banks and the first generation of management, if one can use that term. Hence, important categories of borrowers were, for example, local businessmen of all types, the landed gentry (especially in those regions with large rural estates) and public officials. This also points out that insider lending was a widespread phenomenon in the early savings banks. Considering the

[6] Nygren (1987) and Petersson (2000).

financial system's rather embryonic stage of development and the lack of a public control system aimed at the financial and credit markets, this is in no way surprising. The savings banks and their managers had to trust the social and personal control mechanism to monitor the borrowers in their banks. The savings banks thus in general lacked the necessary resources to monitor and control the borrowers in other ways. Insider lending was, at that time, an accepted and rather well-functioning way of making loans.

The Savings Banks and the Financial Revolution, 1870–1910

From the late 1860s and approximately 50–60 years on, the Swedish financial system, and the whole economy, underwent a remarkable development. This financial revolution was thus intimately related to a parallel industrialization process of the Swedish society. In the beginning of this period, Sweden was one of Europe's poorest and most undeveloped countries. The fast growth rates, especially during the years 1890–1910, turned Sweden into a relatively developed economy (see Table 3.4).

Much of the recent research on Swedish financial history has been devoted to describing and analysing this stage of development, and some of it has taken on the task of empirically testing earlier statements regarding the positive role of the banking system for general economic change and growth. However, Lars Sandberg stated in the late 1970s that an important reason for the successful transformation of the Swedish economy was the growth and liberalization of the financial system from the 1860s. A large number of privately controlled banks—meaning both commercial banks and savings banks—were established, the institutional and organizational boundaries between private and public financial organizations were made clear, and perhaps most importantly, a broad set

Table 3.4 Growth rates of real GDP per head of population, 1820–1913 (annual average compound growth rates)

	Sweden	*Denmark*	*Finland*	*Norway*	*UK*	*Germany*	*France*
1820–1870	0.7	0.9	0.8	0.7	1.2	0.7	0.8
1870–1913	2.0	1.6	1.4	1.3	1.0	1.6	1.5

Source Maddison (1991, p. 49) and Krantz (2000, p. 9)

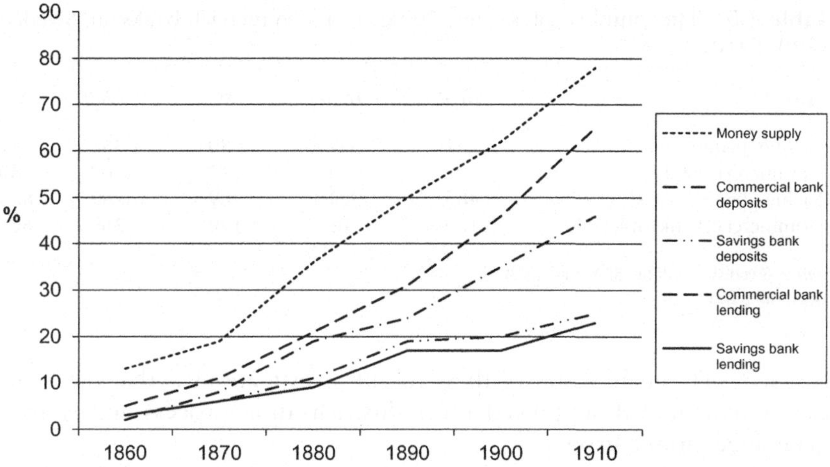

Fig. 3.1 Various financial measures in percent of GDP, 1860–1910 (*Source* Ögren [2009] and Petersson [2001, p. 71])

of new financial services and instruments were introduced and made accessible to the public.[7]

More recent research on the Swedish financial system has further strengthened Sandberg's original arguments and, in addition, linked them up to the growing international debate and discourse on financial revolutions in history.[8] Taking into account both quantitative data (see Fig. 3.1) and more qualitative discussions and results regarding for example the banking system's ability to create liquidity, there is much evidence that there was a financial revolution in Sweden in the latter half of the nineteenth and the early twentieth centuries. The six-fold increase in the money supply, for instance, indicates a profound monetarization of the Swedish economy. Public and businesses of all types and sizes increased their use of paper money, instead of the previously dominating bills of exchange and other forms of promissory notes, as the prevalent means of

[7] Sandberg (1978, 1979). See also Lindgren and Sjögren (2003).

[8] See Rousseau and Sylla (2003).

Table 3.5 The number of savings banks and commercial banks in Sweden, 1870–1910

No. of	*1870*	*1880*	*1890*	*1900*	*1910*
Savings banks	251	347	380	388	441
Commercial banks	36	44	43	67	80
Savings bank offices[a]	485	921	909	748	854
Commercial bank offices[a]	136	205	190	269	625

Source Swedish Banking Statistics, SCB
[a]Including head offices

payment. The main result of these recent investigations is that the financial system indeed supported the industrialization process and spurred general economic growth.[9]

Both the commercial banks and the savings banks naturally played important roles in the financial revolution. Due to the rapidly growing number of newly established banks and branch offices, Sweden soon had a rather dense network of financial intermediaries accessible to the public (see Table 3.5).

The number of savings banks rose very quickly, especially during two separate phases. The first one was in the 1860s and 1870s, when new savings banks were established primarily in the rural areas of the country (see Table 3.6). These savings banks were, in contrast to the earlier savings banks, especially those in the largest towns, first and foremost aimed at providing the local markets, i.e. the agricultural sector, with credit. The deposit activities, and the philanthropic feature that stressed the savings banks' mission to provide help for self-help, were clearly in the background in the rural savings banks. From the very beginning the rural savings banks also developed an exceedingly independent position regarding governmental regulation and intervention. The rural savings banks' tradition of independency and strong local focus, especially regarding the provision of local credit demands, are an important explanation for why a concentration process concerning the whole savings banks movement did not take place until the 1960s.

[9] Ögren (2003, 2006, 2010, 2021). See also Broberg and Ögren (2019) and Hansson and Jonung (1997).

Table 3.6 The geographical location of the savings banks in Sweden, 1870–1910

Year	*In towns*		*In the countryside*		*Total*
	No.	*%*	*No.*	*%*	
1870	82	*33*	169	*67*	251
1880	91	*26*	256	*74*	347
1890	104	*27*	276	*73*	380
1900	103	*27*	285	*73*	388
1910	112	*25*	329	*75*	441

Source Swedish Banking Statistics, SCB

The second wave of new savings banks occurred in the early twentieth century. These new savings banks were mainly situated in the urban areas, and for the first time there could be more than one savings bank in one town. A substantial part of the new savings banks was in fact established as a counter-reaction against the old urban savings banks, which were considered to be very conservative and more adapted to the needs of the middle and upper classes than those of the growing working class. Savings banks that not only aimed their activities towards the urban working classes, but that were also led by their political representatives, were a new feature of the Swedish savings banks from the early twentieth century and on.

There were several proposals to introduce savings bank acts in the 1860s and the early 1870s. However, a massive resistance from the representatives of the rural interests in the Parliament, thus representing the rural savings banks and their struggle for continued independence, effectively stopped such proposals. In 1875, nevertheless, a lenient form of regulation was introduced, i.e. the 1875 savings banks decree. A (small) number of savings banks had gone bankrupt, and the decree stated that all savings banks had to have a reserve fundto cover for losses. Another part of the decree gave the country administrative boards the right to control the savings banks' bookkeeping, and if necessary, to shut a mismanaged savings bank down.[10]

The Savings Bank Act of 1892 was much more extensive and aimed directly at restricting the variety of financial services that the savings banks

[10] Petersson (2001, p. 81).

could offer the public. In many local and regional markets, the savings banks had developed into major deposit and credit organizations and thus competed directly with the commercial banks. For the first time, the term "the natural order", referring to what different kinds of financial organizations were supposed to do and not to do in the eyes of the legislator, was used in the political debate. Advocates of a stricter regulation, who not surprisingly often had own personal economic interests in the well-being of the commercial banks, did not want the savings banks to engage in an "unhealthy competition" with the commercial banks. The savings banks were to be the safest possible alternative for the clients on the deposit markets and should thus not risk the depositor's money by investing for example in loans to business and industry.[11]

Deposit Markets

Beginning with Stockholm's Enskilda Bank in 1856, commercial banks began to get interested in exploiting local and regional deposit markets as a way of funding their lending activities. In 1868, the total deposits in the commercial banks surpassed those in the savings banks for the first time.[12] The savings banks never managed to catch up with the commercial banks again, even if they were close in the interwar years. By 1910 the public's deposits in the commercial banks were almost two times larger than those in the savings banks (see Table 3.7). It is also worth emphasizing that it was the savings banks and the commercial banks that together totally dominated the institutional deposit market in Sweden. They accounted for around 90 per cent of the national market from the 1850s onwards. It was not until the interwar years that other financial organizations, especially the postal office savings banks, the cooperative banks and the insurance companies, managed to establish themselves as credible savings alternate to the savings banks and commercial banks.[13]

The commercial banks soon realized the advantage of offering financial services, especially the possibility of saving, to a broad layer of the public.

[11] Petersson (2001, pp. 82–86) and Sjölander (2003, pp. 59–73).

[12] Commercial banks were from the 1930s allowed to establish in the form of bank with unlimited liability, with the owners being responsible for the banks' all economic activities. It was not until the 1860s that joint stock banks with limited liability were allowed.

[13] Petersson (2001, p. 71).

Table 3.7 Deposits from the public in Swedish banks (market shares in per cent) and total volume of deposits (SEK million), 1870–1910

Year	*Savings banks, %*	*Commercial banks, %*	*Postal office savings banks, %*	*Total volume of deposits, SEK million*
1860	60	40	-	45
1870	44	56	-	131
1880	37	63	-	393
1890	43	55	2	640
1900	35	61	4	1265
1910	35	63	2	2321

Source Swedish Banking Statistics, SCB

Their strategy of engaging in the local deposit markets was intentionally aimed directly at some of the savings banks' traditionally important customers, especially the wealthier private persons and their household savings, including the savings of children. Also, women of all socio-economic classes, who had been so important for the savings banks in the initial stage in the early nineteenth century, were addressed by the commercial banks in their struggle for market shares. And they were obviously successful. For example, in Stockholm's Enskilda Bank, women held 40–50 per cent of the individual deposit accounts in the late nineteenth century.[14]

Credit Markets

The Savings Bank Act of 1892 thus limited the variety of both deposit accounts and credit alternatives that the savings banks could offer the public. The effects on the Swedish institutional credit market were also immediate. The savings bank started to lose market shares to the commercial banks (see Table 3.8).

There was also a change in the investment structure of the savings banks as they were obliged to invest at least 10 per cent of their total deposits in gilt-edged bonds, i.e. government bonds and bonds issued by mortgage institutes. Regarding the loans granted by the savings banks,

[14] Petersson (2006).

Table 3.8 Advances from Swedish banks (market shares in per cent) and total volumes of advances (SEK million), 1870–1910

Year	*Savings banks, %*	*Commercial banks, %*	*The National Bank, %*	*Total volume of bank advances, SEK million*	*Total volume of the institutional credit market[a], SEK million*
1870	26	55	19	221	415
1875	26	62	12	424	699
1880	26	61	13	474	827
1885	28	61	11	681	1106
1890	31	58	11	787	1255
1895	31	60	9	931	1397
1900	25	67	8	1558	2104
1905	25	67	8	2180	2784
1910	24	69	7	2982	3808

Source Nygren (1985) and Swedish Banking Statistics, SCB
[a]Including mortgage institutes, the National Debt Office and insurance companies

there was a shift towards mortgages as the dominating form of collateral in the late nineteenth century. Many savings banks now had to deal with hundreds of loan applicationsevery year, and it simply became more difficult, and too expensive in terms of transaction costs, to monitor large volumes of loans secured by name, i.e. personal guarantee. In 1875 there was also a change in the laws concerning mortgages and the legal ratification of estates which made it considerably easier, and cheaper, than before to give loans on mortgage. In the early twentieth century, less than 20 per cent of the collateral was in the form of personal guarantees.[15]

Some savings banks continued to engage in the financing of local business and industry even after the Savings Bank Act of 1892, especially in the newly industrialized cities in the north of Sweden, but the general trend was still a change towards more long term and delimited lending operations. As the shift in collateral suggests, mortgages gradually became the hallmark of the savings banks' lending operations, a hallmark that persisted throughout the entire twentieth century.

[15] Petersson (2001, pp. 76–78).

Conclusion

The early, mostly urban, Swedish savings banks were important for the general development of the banking and financial system. The savings banks were market makers on numerous local markets and had a role in the formation of banking, although several of the savings banks were quite small. Especially in developing local deposit markets, savings banks played a significant role. Many savings banks were also active in financing local businesses, trade and industry.

Insider lending, personal networks and cooperation between savings banks and commercial banks were distinct features of the early banking system. Hence, the founding fathers of the savings banks and the first generation of "managers" had to make extensive use of their personal networks in making investment decisions in their savings banks. Obviously, in the savings banks both societal and public interests on the one hand, and private, profit seeking interests on the other hand, could join forces. The results were mutually beneficent.

The early savings banks in Sweden were almost entirely free from governmental regulation and supervision, with one important exception. If a savings bank wanted to be exempted from governmental tax, and thus be classified as a charitable organization, its charters had to be sent to and approved by the government in Stockholm. Consequently, and being very aware of the more and more positive connotation associated with the term "savings bank", almost every savings bank from this time on followed that formal procedure. This naturally further strengthened the savings banks' legitimacy as reliable financial organizations and explains, at least partially, why the general public chose to trust the savings banks with their savings.

The savings banks played an important role in the stage of economic development that in the Swedish case included both a financial and an industrial revolution. The savings banks contributed by collecting large volumes of deposits from a broad layer of the population and transforming them into loans. In many local credit markets, especially the smaller ones both in rural areas and in small and medium-sized cities, the savings banks and the commercial banks cooperated rather than competed. As a result, many local bank-industry networks were established, based on both formal relations, such as credit contracts, and more informal, personal relations. Very often a small group of individuals filled all the strategic positions both in the banks and in the companies that were customers in the banks. The rather intimate relationship with the commercial banks continued to be an important part of many savings banks' everyday business (see Fig. 3.2).

However, the personal networks between savings banks and commercial banks started to loosen up in the early twentieth century, due to several factors. One is that the commercial banks no longer had the need to engage savings banks in the distribution of their own bank notes, as the National Bank was given exclusive right to issue bank notes in the early twentieth century. Another reason is that many savings banks became more professional organizations. From the late nineteenth century, not only the large savings banks in the cities, but also the smaller and rural savings banks in general had the resources to hire fulltime employees.

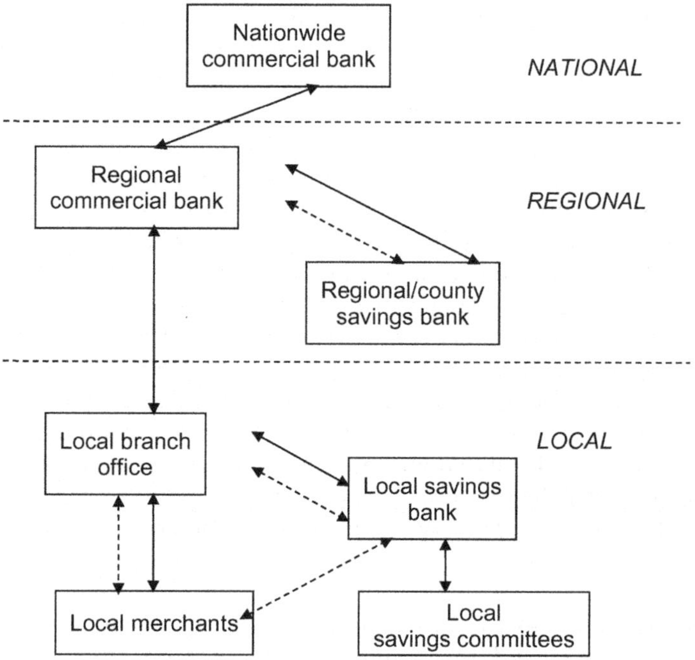

Fig. 3.2 The formal and informal relationships between commercial banks and savings bank in the late nineteenth century Sweden (*Note* Continuous line = formal relation, for example different kind of contractual credit agreements. Dotted line = informal relation, for example interlocking directorates)

References

Andersson, B. (1983), "Early History of Banking in Gothenburg Discount House Operations 1783–1818". *Scandinavian Economic History Review*, Vol. XXXI, pp. 50–67.

Broberg, O., & Ögren, A. (2019), "Names, Shares and Mortgages: The Formalisation of Swedish Commercial Bank Lending, 1870–1938". *Financial History Review*, Vol. 26, pp. 81–108.

Hansson, P., & Jonung, L. (1997), "Finance and Economic Growth. The Case of Sweden 1834–1991", Working paper no. 176, The Economic Research Institute, Stockholm School of Economics.

Hellgren, H. (2003), *Fasta förbindelser. En studie av låntagare hos sparbanken och informella kreditgivare i Sala 1860–1910*. Uppsala: Acta Universitatis Upsaliensis.

Karlsson, M., & Petersson, T. (2006), "Banking or Philanthropy? The Development and Characteristics of the Nineteenth Century Scandinavian Savings Banks". *Revue d'Histoire Nordique / Nordic Historical Review*, Vol. 2, pp. 167–192.

Kärrlander, T. (2013), "Malmö diskont 1817: An Institutional Analysis of a Banking Crisis". *Financial History Review*, Vol. 20, pp. 163–182.

Krantz, O. (2000), "Svensk ekonomisk tillväxt under 1900-talet". *Ekonomisk Debatt*, Vol. 28, pp. 7–15.

Lilja, K. (2004), *Marknad och hushåll. Sparande och krediter i Falun 1820–1910 utifrån ett livscykelperspektiv*. Uppsala: Acta Universitatis Upsaliensis.

Lindgren, H. (2002), "The Modernization of Swedish Credit Markets, 1840–1905: Evidence from Probate Records". *The Journal of Economic History*, Vol. 62, Issue 3, pp. 810–832.

Lindgren, H., & Sjögren, H. (2003), "Banking Systems as "Ideal Types" and Political Economy. The Swedish Case, 1820–1914". In D. Forsyth & D. Verdier (Eds.), *Gerschenkron Revisited. The Political Origins of Banking Structures*. Oxford: Oxford University Press.

Maddison, A. (1991), *Dynamic Forces in Capitalist Development. A Long-Run Comparative View*. Oxford: Oxford University Press.

Nygren, I. (1983), "Transformation of Bank Structures in the Industrial Period: The Case of Sweden 1820–1913". *Journal of European Economic History*, Vol. 12, pp. 29–68.

Nygren, I. (1985), *Från Stockholms Banco till Citibank. Svensk kreditmarknad under 325 år*. Malmö: Liber förlag.

Nygren, I. (1987), *Göteborgs kreditmarknad 1820–1913*. Department of Economic History, Gothenburg University.

Ögren, A. (2003), *Empirical Studies in Money, Credit and Banking: The Swedish Credit Market in Transition, 1834–1913*. Stockholm: Stockholm School of Economics.

Ögren, A. (2006), "Free or Central Banking? Liquidity and Financial Deepening in Sweden, 1834-1913". *Explorations in Economic History*, Vol. 43, pp. 64–93.

Ögren, A. (2009), "Financial Revolution and Economic Modernization in Sweden". *Financial History Review*, Vol. 16, pp. 47–71.

Ögren, A. (2010) (Ed.), *The Swedish Financial Revolution*. New York: Palgrave Macmillan.

Ögren, A. (2021), "The Political Economy of Banking Regulation: Interest Groups and Rational Choice in the Formation of the Swedish Banking System 1822-1921". *Business History*, Vol. 63, pp. 271–291.

Perlinge, A. (2005), *Sockenbankirerna. Kreditrelationer och tidig bankverksamhet. Vånga socken i Skåne 1840–1900*. Stockholm: Nordiska museets förlag.

Petersson, T. (2000), "Playing It Safe? Lending Policies of the Savings Bank in Nyköping, 1832–1875". In L. Fälting et al., *Both a Borrower and a Lender Be. Savings Banks in the Economic Development of Sweden 1820–1939*, Uppsala Papers in Financial History, no. 12, Uppsala University, Uppsala.

Petersson, T. (2001), *Framväxten av ett lokalt banksystem. Oppunda sparbank, Södermanlands enskilda bank och stationssamhället Katrineholm 1850–1916*. Uppsala: Acta Universitatis Upsaliensis.

Petersson, T. (2006), "The Silent Partners. Women, Capital and the Development of the Financial System in Nineteenth-Century Sweden". In R. Beachy, B. Craig, & A. Owens (Eds.), *Rethinking Separate Spheres. Women, Business and Finance in Nineteenth-Century Europe*. London & New York: Berg Publishers.

Rousseau, P. L., & Sylla, R. (2003), "Financial Systems, Economic Growth and Globalization". In M. D. Bordo & J. G. Williamson (Eds.), *Globalization in Historical Perspective*. Chicago: University of Chicago Press.

Sandberg, L (1978), "Banking and Economic Growth in Sweden Before World War I". *The Journal of Economic History*, Vol. XXXVIII, pp. 650–680.

Sandberg, L (1979), "The Case of the Impoverished Sophisticate: Human Capital and Swedish Economic Growth Before World War I". *Journal of Economic History*, Vol. XXXIX, pp. 225–241.

Sjölander, A. (2003), *Den naturliga ordningen. Makt och intressen i de svenska sparbankerna 1882–1968*. Uppsala: Acta Universitatis Upsaliensis.

Swedish Banking Statistics, SCB (Statistics Sweden).

CHAPTER 4

Savers and the Risk of Deposit Banking

Abstract The issue to be discussed is how financial organizations manage to attract savings. The chapter shows that deposit banking in Sweden was introduced in the savings banks and for many decades functioned with restrained legislation and control of the state. However, personal trustworthiness and founders' network had limits in building and supporting legitimacy. When deposit banking increased during the second half of the nineteenth century, bank regulations were introduced to secure account holders' deposits.

Keywords Attract depositors · Legitimacy without regulation · Competition · Savings banks

This chapter will discuss how early financial organizations managed to attract savings. How did they handle the risks with deposits? Swedish savings banks were "market makers on the savings arena", but they also managed to adapt to a changing business environment during industrialization and the financial (r)evolution.[1] How was it possible for local embryonic savings organizations to develop into modern deposit banks

[1] Ögren (2010) and Lilja (2010).

M. Larsson et al., *Risk Management in Early Banking*, Palgrave Studies in the History of Finance,
https://doi.org/10.1007/978-3-030-80775-7_4

during the period 1820–1910? And how was trust between savings banks and depositors built and preserved? In the following chapter, early deposit banking is analysed and examples from other countries are discussed. As will be shown, the development in the deposit market arena in Sweden had more of an incremental development rather than radical change and the savings banks had an important role in this process during the period studied.

How to Create Legitimacy Without Regulation?

In the beginning of the nineteenth century, the Swedish financial system was underdeveloped. The public's low trust in the banking sector was more or less a consequence of the poor experiences connected to the failures of the Discount Banks in the 1810s (Chapter 3). These privately owned financial organizations had, during the recession following the Napoleonic Wars, turned out to be just as risky as the business of private bankers. As formal regulation protecting depositors were not in place, and deposits in these banks were lost in the bankruptcies in 1818. From then on the National Bank (*Riksbanken*) was the only actor. As its operations were located in the largest towns, the alternatives to deposit banking were almost non-existent. Most inhabitants predominately had no (or bad) experiences with deposit banking. In this context, the government recognized the recommendation of establishing savings banks as a solution to poverty. By emphasizing this philanthropic character, savings banks were not to be linked to banks that had commercial interests.

Having strong contact with the local society was important for the savings banks to become well-functioning and trustful organizations. The Skogman report expressed that it was a matter for the local communities—not for the central State—to establish such banks (see also Chapter 3). The report also gave clear instructions regarding how to organize savings banks and, in detail, outlined how to handle deposits, depositors and savings banks' accounts.[2] The Skogman report was sent to public officials and authorities all over the country and was considered a recommendation. By making it possible for less-wealthy groups to deposit their savings into a savings bank, it was believed that the problems with

[2] Skogman (1819).

rising costs for poor relief could be mitigated. Savings banks were considered to be possible solutions to poverty as well as instruments for thrifty behaviour.[3] The savings funds (*Sparkassor*), which had been established at proto-industries in some parts of Sweden already at the beginning of the nineteenth century, also shared these ideas.[4]

The Swedish savings banks were originally supposed to be philanthropic mutual non-profit and local organizations founded in larger towns from the 1820s onwards. The initiators were among the local elite who inspired confidence through their official positions as governors, mayors and other public officials in the state or the church. Several of these people also belonged to the economic elite (noblemen, merchants and artisans) and had good knowledge of financial matters. Some of them most likely had a history as a creditor or even a 'private banker'.[5] The founders thus represented more of a continuity than a change during a period when the financial system was undeveloped.

The Skogman report had stipulated that it was convenient to have 'admittedly honest, benevolent and wealthy persons' in charge of running the savings banks so there was no doubt regarding the safety of deposits. The founding fathers had to take on the roles of economic guarantors for the savings banks; it was also understood that unselfish consideration always, without exception, guided their work.[6] The founders' socio-economic position and status as local authorities gave the savings banks legitimacy.[7] Moreover, the founders were often also involved in several social commitments during the period studied. This was, for example, the case of the volunteer assignments of the local elite society that DBW mentioned in Chapter 1. Establishing a school and a savings bank was among the tasks that this society recognized as being important in the

[3] Lilja (2000, pp. 35–37) and Bäcklund and Lilja (2014, p. 618).

[4] These savings funds were inspired by models in Sachsen, Germany. Sommarin (1940, pp. 15–17). Several of these saving funds would later on cease and move deposits to the local savings bank. Cronbladh (1993).

[5] Private bankers were often local trusted "asset managers" that both lent money and accepted deposits. Perlinge (2005).

[6] Skogman (1819, pp. 9–10). The savings banks phenomenon was part of liberal and paternalistic ideas of the need to establish organisations that could support the less-wealthy individuals' "help-to-self-help". Lilja (2000, pp. 29–31).

[7] This was also the case in other countries as for example France, Américi (2002, pp. 5–19).

strategy to fight poverty.[8] These idealistic descriptions of the founding fathers were of great significance as they markedly strengthened the philanthropic characteristics of the savings banks.

The early savings banks were introduced and functioned with restrained legislation and control by the state. However, this strong dependence and the fact that the founders and these local elite often were civil servants meant that the savings banks were considered patriarchal, semi-public institutions in the local community. For a long time, savings banks in Sweden were under the legislation of local funds founded out of social motives.[9] These organizations, moreover, also sometimes shared board members. This probably gave savings banks legitimacy already from the beginning. It might have been important for depositors to recognize them for their well-known founders when deciding to open a savings banks account.

Swedish savings banks were similar to their Scottish and English role models. They all were inspired by the ideas that were formulated in 'Essay on the Nature and Advantage of Parish Banks' (1815).[10] The charters that were recommended in the publication, and were used to organize the savings banks, focused on deposits and clearly outlined the advantages of saving regularly. The essay emphasized the importance of an interest rate on deposits that was considered appropriately high. A clear point was that very small deposits were also to have a relatively high-interest rate, attracting depositors from the target group of less-wealthy individuals. Additionally, bonuses were given to frequent savers.[11] These ideas were more or less duplicated in the Skogman report, which was the guide for founding local savings banks all over Sweden.[12]

From the very start, the individual savings banks in Sweden had detailed charters for their operations. These published charters brought

[8] Karlsson (2012).

[9] For example, church funds, school funds and poor relief funds. *Underdånigt betänkande angående Sveriges ekonomiska och finansiella utveckling under åren 1834–1860* (1863, pp. 72–74).

[10] The text was written by Minister Henry Duncan, Ruthwell, Scotland. Horne (1947, pp. 1–2 and 43–50).

[11] The interest rate of 4–5 per cent was recommended by Duncan. It also became the recommendation for the early savings banks in Sweden. Horne (1947, p. 45) and Skogman (1819, pp. 10–17).

[12] Skogman (1819).

clarity, predictability and transparency to customers, and probably reduced the uncertainty regarding the safety of savings.[13] Standardized and publicized terms most certainly increased the attractiveness of these new organizations. This was something that normally was lacking when dealing with private bankers and other actors on the (private) credit market.

Working with well-defined target groups of less-wealthy individuals meant that the Swedish savings banks also accepted small deposits. Savers could make deposits for up to ten years, or even twenty years, with terms defined in advance.[14] When this goal of saving was reached, the savings banks had fulfilled their obligations and the account holder had to close the account.

As savings banks aimed for the long-term accumulation of savings, withdrawals were highly restricted. Account holders had to notify the bank before making withdrawals, thereby ensuring that the bank could give the account holder the requested amount.[15] This also, importantly, established that the withdrawal was not done with too great ease. The aim of the savings banks was not the only motivator; reducing the risks with the difficulties for the savings banks' staff to manage highly fluctuating deposits was also critical.

The aim of the savings banks was obvious and transparent because of these strict instructions. This focus on providing important information about saving in these banks showed financial responsibility and trustworthiness. To prevent wealthier persons from taking advantage of savings banks, maximum levels for a single deposit as well as for total deposits on savings accounts were strictly regulated.[16] Setting maximum levels was also motivated by the great effort to administer savings. Finding borrowers or investors that accepted paying an interest of six per cent was a problem for some savings banks at times. They, therefore, decided to change their charters, thereby more strictly restricting the geographical

[13] Lilja (2004, pp. 52 and 102).

[14] Skogman (1819, pp. 10–11) and Silow (1926, p. 238).

[15] Lilja (2000, p. 34).

[16] Horne (1947, p. 45) and Lilja (2004, p. 102).

area of activity.[17] Introducing firmer instructions in the charters regarding how to organize the undertakings within the savings banks was, for some banks, also a result of the founders' sometimes low commitment in the daily operations.[18] The necessary changes in the charters in both of these situations were probably crucial for the possibility of upholding a well-functioning organization and the survival of these savings banks.

Swedish savings banks, like their Scottish and English counterparts, were established out of a social motive. A difference was, however, that Swedish savings banks partly managed deposits differently from British savings banks. Instead of placing the capital with the National bank, as was recommended in the Scottish and English examples, the Swedish savings banks already acted as lenders on the local credit market from the beginning.[19] This was also the praxis among the many different funds operating in the local community. This strong local affiliation was probably seen as both natural and desirable for many depositors. Keeping managed deposits 'within sight' was also most certainly a strategy to lower the credit risks for these kinds of organizations during a period of few regulations in the financial sector.

By the middle of the nineteenth century, many Swedish towns had a savings bank while commercial banks were operating in larger towns. At this time, establishing savings banks in rural areas became popular as well. The founders were aware that savings banks were an important element in the local infrastructure. Geographical closeness to the bank improved the possibilities for individuals from the target groups to open a bank account. Consequently, when founding savings banks in the countryside, the early savings banks' charters were copied. This was a strategy to minimize the risks when establishing a new organization.

[17] Some savings banks had difficulties to find lenders that were interested to pay the necessary level of interest needed, considering the decision to pay five per cent of interest on deposits. Lilja (2000, p. 34).

[18] Lilja (2000, p. 35).

[19] Skogman (1819, pp. 15–17 and 47–48), for example, Silow (1926, p. 242).

How Do Banks Attract Depositors?

Savings banks were intended to foster habits of thrift and foresight.[20] Even a low-income worker was believed to be able to accumulate sufficient funds to escape poverty.[21] Studies from different countries during the nineteenth century indicate that workers were savers when possible. Precautionary savings dominated.[22] Many blue-collar workers were, however, too poor to have any surplus. Consequently, they had difficulties saving. As a result, most of the early savings banks in Sweden experienced fluctuations in their operations as withdrawals were almost as frequent as deposits.[23] It became difficult to establish a stable business and, consequently, the risks with deposit banking were high.

The expansion of savings banks progressed slowly during the first half of the nineteenth century in Sweden (Table 4.2). In order to force the target groups to make deposits, some employers in the early phase of the savings banks chose to put (part of) of their employees' wages in a savings banks' account. There are several examples of employers opening accounts for (mostly) their (female) servants. Another example was when workers in the copper mine in the town of Falun had to accept that a part of their wage increase in the 1820s and the early 1830s was placed at a savings banks' account.[24] The latter might explain why a large share of the new accounts in the savings bank in Falun, already from the early years, belonged to blue-collar workers (Table 4.1).

Despite lacking surplus, it seems as if small savers found their way to the savings bank; between one-third and one-half of all accounts belonged to blue-collar workers during the first half of the nineteenth century (Table 4.1). This development of increasing numbers of accounts (Table 4.2) and workers' obvious trust in these organizations was probably, as mentioned above, a result of the detailed and pedagogically formulated charters as well as the founders' status as well-known individuals in the local community. It might, of course, also have been a consequence of

[20] For example, Kiesewetter (1981).

[21] For example, Fishlow (1961, p. 26), Américi (2002, p. 19) and Wadhwani (2002, pp. 43–44).

[22] Johnson (1985), Boyer (2009, pp. 62–79), Payne (1967, pp. 157–171), Schulz (1981, p. 493) and Lilja and Bäcklund (2016).

[23] Lilja (2004, p. 103), *Varifrån kommer, hur uppstår sparkapitalet?* (1946, pp. 66–70).

[24] Lilja (2000, pp. 49–50).

Table 4.1 Account holders' socio-economic status in three Swedish savings banks, per cent

Savings bank	*Year*	*No. of account holders*	*High and middle strata, %*	*Workers, %*	*Total, %*
Stockholm	1830	1104	49	51	100
	1893	2467	33	67	100
DBV	1830	262	73	27	100
	1839	453	65	35	100
	1848	991	48	52	100
	1860	2662	36	64	100
Falun (Only new depositors)	1830–33	262	24	76	100
	1855	138	35	65	100
	1880	150	34	66	100

Sources *Varifrån kommer, hur uppstår sparkapitalet?* (1946, pp. 57 and 78), Karlsson (2012, pp. 125–129) and Lilja (2004, pp. 107 and 122)

Table 4.2 Number of accounts, total deposits, and average balances of savings banks (SB) and commercial banks (CB), 1834–1910, SEK

Year	*Number of accounts, thousands*		*Total deposits, million SEK*		*Average balance, SEK*	
	SB	*CB*	*SB*	*CB*	*SB*	*CB*
1834[a]	23		2	0	102	–
1840	48	–	5	1	108	–
1850	100	–	13	1	129	–
1860	188	–	27	18	145	–
1870	354	36	57	74	162	2084
1880	762	128	146	247	177	1919 (158)[b]
1890	1073	104	275	352	256	1930 (275)[b]
1900	1229	448	437	772	334	1724 (494)[b]
1910	1560	806	809	1466	541	1818 (382)[b]

Sources Swedish Banking Statistics, SCB
Note [a]Data missing for 1830. [b]Average balance on savings accounts (*Sparkasseräkning*)

the lack of failures among savings banks in Sweden. Deposits at a savings bank's account were most certainly more or less considered to lack risk. Moreover, it meant a rather good return on (also small) deposits during a period when (financial) saving alternatives were few.

The charters were adjusted in several ways over the years to assist the demand of depositors and to make the savings banks more attractive. Modifications increased accessibility as well as the interest of having a bank account. Operating hours were extended from the original two hours during the weekend to several hours a week. Clerks were also employed. Moreover, the maximum levels of savings banks' accounts were raised and withdrawals were made easier. These changes meant that it became easier for the account holders to keep their accounts over a longer period.[25] The development was also a necessary step towards establishing more professional organizations. The savings banks were seen as good examples. As a result, the number of savings banks grew steadily from the middle of the nineteenth century (Table 3.1). The expansion of savings banks made most inhabitants accustomed to the statements of the virtues of having a savings account and deposit banking.

Studies show that in 1860 blue-collar workers constituted one-half of the account holders, although this group of account holders had just one-third of total deposits.[26] Instead, a large share of the account holders belonged to the middle class (Table 4.1). Several other countries experienced similar overrepresentations of different wealth levels among account holders at this time.[27] Accumulated capital in the Swedish savings banks had increased largely from deposits by wealthier groups.[28] However, when real wages started to increase from the 1870s onward, a growing number of the savings banks' target groups had the economic possibilities to save. British studies show that when economic circumstances for workers in general improved at the end of the nineteenth century, bank deposits greatly increased.[29] This development was also shown for Swedish workers during the same period.[30]

From the early 1870s, the commercial banks also offered deposits on savings accounts, a category of accounts that was directly comparable with the only account category that the savings banks could offer (Table

[25] Lilja (2004, pp. 104–106).

[26] Sommarin (1942, p. 148).

[27] For example, Fishlow (1961), Alter et al. (1994, pp. 744–766), Ross (2001, pp. 305–309), Olmstead (1975), Ó Gráda (2003, pp. 34–38) and Maltby (2011).

[28] Nygren (1981, pp. 84–89).

[29] Boyer (2009, pp. 67–72).

[30] Bäcklund and Lilja (2014) and Lilja and Bäcklund (2016).

4.2). A growing number of account holders from the middle class and better-off blue-collar workers, the small-scale savers that were supposed to be the typical depositor in the savings banks, at least in the eyes of the governmental regulators, from now on held an account in commercial banks. As accounts in commercial banks traditionally were company accounts or belonged to wealthier individuals, the average balances in the commercial banks' accounts decreased (Table 4.2). However, deposit banking was not the main business concept of these banks: it was to give credit. Considering that commercial banks often shared board members with the local savings bank, they had learnt how to organize deposit banking for the masses.[31] Nevertheless, being financial company was related to risk-taking. More risk-averse individuals probably preferred low-risk organizations like, for example, savings banks.

During the latter half of the nineteenth century, it seems as if many urban Swedish workers had been savings banks' account holders at some time in their lives. Many young and unmarried (often female) persons opened an account when they started working.[32] Although most of the accounts were short term,[33] some workers accumulated savings over a long period.[34] In this regard, there were significant gender differences as well as variances between married and unmarried individuals. A Scottish study shows that savings banks' accounts were used for families' needs for recurrent payment obligations, such as rent.[35] The family's economic obligations also seem to have motivated the opening of savings banks' accounts among male workers in Sweden. The husband's account was normally used for family purposes. Sometimes, the wife also had a savings bank's account. Two accounts or more could be justified if the family wanted to save more than was acceptable on one account according to the regulated maximum levels. This was a well-known practice in most countries.[36] Deposit banking was obviously a family matter.

[31] Nygren (1985, pp. 48 and 54), Petersson (2001, pp. 134–13) and Sjölander (2003, p. 84).

[32] Lilja and Bäcklund (2016, pp. 111–132).

[33] For example, Alter et al. (1994), Wadhwani (2002, p. 50) and Lilja (2004, pp. 109–113).

[34] Haber and Gratton (1993, pp. 72–81).

[35] Ross (2013, pp. 195–196).

[36] Lilja (2004, pp. 116–117) and Ó Gráda (2003, pp. 42–46).

There is, however, also an indication that married women's accounts were sometimes for individual use. Studies from England interpret that married women "were active economic agents in their own right"[37] by the middle of the nineteenth century and used saving through these bank accounts as insurance for future needs.[38] In Sweden, female savers constituted an important share of the account holders in the savings banks from the 1820s, despite having no formal right to decide in economic questions (widows being the exception); approximately one-half of all account holders were adult women.[39] Women in general saved much more in savings banks than men in the same socio-economic category, both in absolute and in relative terms; women's accounts were more often long-lasting as well.[40] Women tended to outlive men and consequently the widow had to save for old age.[41] All in all, it made women a relatively stable and important group of savers in the savings banks and deposit banking.

Female deposits were of most importance for investments during industrialization and to aid in the growth of the domestic economy.[42] Research has shown that women at this time seem to have preferred low-risk investment areas. Investments could be said to be gender divided. In Britain in the 1910s, female investors appear to have preferred to avoid risk-taking if possible.[43] They sought secure investments and often "remained relatively passive in relation to their financial dealing".[44] They were considered to be "financial investors primarily seeking a *rentier*

[37] Perriton (2012, p. 12).

[38] Maltby (2011), Perriton (2012) and Perriton and Maltby (2015).

[39] The Swedish Code of 1734 placed women (widows excluded) under the legal framework of their father, brother or husband. In 1858 unmarried women were gradually removed from legal incapacity and in 1884 then the age of majority became 21 years. In 1874, it became possible for married women to control their property. They also gained the right to dispose their own income and private property. Lilja (2004, p. 25).

[40] The balances of women's savings accounts were often 20–30 per cent higher than men's. Petersson (2006, p. 43) and Lilja (2004, p. 117).

[41] For the ages 55 and above, an age when many women had become widows, the average female depositor once again saved considerably more than male depositors of the same age. Lilja (2004). See also Perlinge (2005, pp. 110–111).

[42] Petersson (2006) and Owens (2006).

[43] Maltby and Rutterford (2006, pp. 220–253).

[44] Owens (2006, p. 25).

Table 4.3 Adult depositors in six large Swedish savings banks

Savings bank	*Year*	*No. of depositors*	*Women %*	*Of which were, %*				*Total, %*
				Widows	*Wives*	*Unmarried*	*Servants*[c]	
Stockholm	1821	644	47	7	13	28	52	100
	1832–41[a]	865	52	11	16	34	39	100
	1842–61[b]	1709	52	9	20	32	39	100
Falun	1830–33[b]	231	32	10	8	22	45	100
	1855[b]	96	58	16	18	11	50	100
Borås	1831–32	135	51	6	13	29	52	100
	1841	541	47	2	10	58	30	100
	1855	1216	49	10	11	19	60	100
Nyköping	1832–62[b]	2115	44	19	9	29	43	100
Jönköping	1839	1165	50	17	0	34	49	100
Sölvesborg	1860	662	52	17	7	26	50	100

Source *Varifrån kommer, hur uppstår sparkapitalet?* (1946), Lilja (2000), Almén (1930), Danielsson (1931), Björnstedt (1939), accounting records of Nyköping's savings bank
Note [a]Annual averages of new depositors. [b]New depositors. [c]Also unmarried

income".[45] Moreover, women were, according to the study, interested in areas in which they had access to information and investments were considered secure and returns reliable.[46] These considerations might have been important for women in general at this time. It most surely made deposit banking in savings banks attractive.

The combination of needs and lack of alternatives probably also explains why savings banks were important for unmarried women from all socio-economic strata.[47] Few unskilled (male) workers held an account, while domestic (female) servants were one of the largest single groups of account holders in the savings banks in Sweden (Table 4.3). This was also the case in many other countries at this time.[48] During the nineteenth century, every second female account holder in the Swedish

[45] Owens (2006, p. 25).

[46] Owens (2006, p. 26).

[47] Lilja and Bäcklund (2016, p. 126).

[48] Fishlow (1961, pp. 28–29 and 36). See also, Lilja (2004, pp. 116–126).

savings banks was a servant while a majority (often between 70 and 75 per cent) was between 16 and 25 years of age and unmarried. Many of the females belonged to the growing number of unmarried women of middle class, individuals who also saved in commercial banks. Unmarried female savers were, in fact, one of the most industrious groups of savers. They saved more than twice the amount as men of the same age and marital status. Female depositors in the savings banks also saved more continuously and on a long-term basis. Consequently, in some cases, these women managed to accumulate amounts corresponding to an annual salary of a male worker in industry.[49] Presumably, most of these unmarried women wished to marry and settle down in the future.[50] There is some evidence suggesting that once the young female depositor got married, the savings within the family were transferred to the husband's accounts. If the woman did not marry, she could use her capital for old age. For this reason, the practice that women could use their savings banks' accounts according to their own wishes was of most importance.

From the bank's point of view, the female depositors must have been the ultimate customers. They were loyal, saved large amounts on a long-term basis and very seldom, if at all, made any demands to gain influence, for example regarding how the banks were managed and who were granted loans, in correlation to their actual importance to the deposit banks.

Children under the age of 16 were continuously an important category of depositors during the nineteenth century, making up approximately one-fourth of all accounts in the savings banks in Sweden. The possibility to save for children was, in fact, one of the main ideas of the savings banks from the very beginning. Since it was the parents or other legal guardians that opened and administered accounts for children, the children naturally often came from the middle and upper socio-economic classes. Also, workers seem to have prioritized accounts for their children if possible. It is important to highlight that an account, in many cases, was opened for each child in the family despite gender. Children's accounts were influenced by parents wanting to give them economic support when they left home. This also explains why withdrawals on children's accounts were only done in exceptional cases and then, not surprisingly, mostly

[49] Lilja (2004, pp. 116–126).

[50] Alter et al. (1994, p. 738) and Lilja (2004, pp. 123–126).

among account holders belonging to the less-wealthy groups. Children's accounts often lasted for a long time: on average more than ten years. Several of them continued to save with a savings banks' account as adults.[51] Accepting small deposits, having low risks and reliable returns were advantages with the savings banks when parents decided to open savings accounts for children. Attracting the more wealthy groups and their children were most certainly important for the long-term stability and survival of the savings banks. It also contributed to strengthen the legitimacy of savings banks and the idea of them as trustful and low-risk organizations.

Deposit Banking in a Changing Market

In Sweden, deposit banking expanded quickly during the industrial take-off from the 1870s onwards as a result of monetization, industrialization and economic growth. Most savings banks now reformed their charters to improve them to meet changing terms on the deposit market. They successively chose to open for all groups in society and maximum amounts for deposits were raised as operations were forced to adjust to growing wealth and a more competitive market for savings. Moreover, the interest rate on deposits—that had been kept for decades—was modified downward.[52] As a consequence of these reforms, the savings banks previous guise as savings funds faded. Still, the most distinct characteristics of the savings banks—being a non-profit organization controlled by a board with a strong local affiliation—were preserved. However, being philanthropic associations meant that savings banks could not be regulated as either banks or associations; the latter classification was how they were viewed in, for example, Great Britain.[53]

The fast expansion of the number of savings banks led the Swedish Parliament to formulate a first national ordinance in 1875. It was decided that the county administrative board was given the right to inspect the local savings banks accounts.[54] The effort to regulate savings banks was

[51] Lilja (2004, pp. 117–118 and 123–124), *Varifrån kommer, hur uppstår sparkapitalet?* (1946, pp. 12 and 80).

[52] Lilja (2000, pp. 52–57).

[53] Horne (1947, pp. 71–80).

[54] Sjölander (2003, pp. 16 and 60–62).

motivated by them now administering large and fast-growing deposits (Table 4.2). It probably was also a result of the increasing competition from the commercial banks along with these banks having many influential representatives in the Parliament with an interest in distinguishing savings banks from other deposit banks.[55] As the ordinance in 1875 was considered to be a recommendation, it had little real impact on the savings banks. For the development of the savings banks' organizations, a more significant change was that several of them had decided to include a member from the local representative assembly in the savings banks' boards after the municipal law of 1862.[56] This was an important step away from savings banks being considered philanthropic institutions and towards becoming more formalized organizations with representatives selected due to competence. This new way of electing members of the savings banks' boards over time most certainly increased their legitimacy as being professional financial organizations.

The legal control of the Swedish savings banks was finally set with the savings banks' law of 1892. It was stressed in this law that the savings banks' main purpose was to accept deposits from the public. As savings banks' operations were, in many ways, already in accordance with the law, it meant no major changes for most savings banks. The law stipulated the terms on savings banks' lending as a way of avoiding hazardous management of deposits and, consequently, bank failures. It clarified the differences between savings banks, savings funds and commercial banks. The law reduced the diversity between actors in deposit banking that had developed over time and thus was already established in the late nineteenth century.[57]

The serious parliamentary critique of the Swedish savings banks not reaching their main target groups of workers and servants led to the founding of the Post Office Savings Banks (POSB) in 1884. POSB were, by the end of the nineteenth century, established in several of the industrialized countries. They were to improve accessibility as well as continuity of savings if the account holder moved. These public facilities, organized within the post offices, were founded in Sweden on the same principles as the savings banks. However, a state guarantee and the supervision of the

[55] Sjölander (2003, pp. 60–62).

[56] Lilja (2010, pp. 51–52).

[57] Sjölander (2003, pp. 18–20) and Petersson (2001, pp. 82–86).

government likely increased the legitimacy of these POSB. Considering that the state was the ultimate guarantor for deposits, it was probably attractive to open an account in the POSB. Nevertheless, as the interest rate on savings was relatively low, the POSB did not become a success related to deposit banking for some years to come. Already from the start, the operation costs of the Swedish POSB were huge and the interest level on deposits was on average 0.75 per cent lower than in most savings banks. The numbers of account holders in the POSB were 237,000 in 1890 and 557,000 in 1910. It meant that the POSB never surpassed savings banks in deposits or the number of depositors, notwithstanding them having many offices (post offices all over the country) and long opening hours.[58] However, the average amount on accounts was smaller and total deposits only amounted to 5–10 per cent of total deposits in the savings banks these years.[59] This indicates that POSB, to a greater extent than savings banks, managed to reach people with limited means. This was also the case in Great Britain, where the average amount on POSB savings accounts was half that of Trustee Savings Bank.[60]

Deposit Banking and Depositors

The rising number of actors in deposit banking led to approximately one out of every four Swedish inhabitants having a savings bank account and one out of seven having an account in a commercial bank in 1910 (Table 4.2). As workers in general were better off at the end of the nineteenth century in Sweden, they now managed to constitute a larger portion of the account holders in the savings banks (Table 4.1). This development of increasing numbers of account holders from the working class was also observed in several other countries at this time. In Britain, approximately 40 per cent of working-class financial funds in 1901 were deposited in savings banks.[61] However, British workers net savings rates were still low

[58] Samuelsson (1978, pp. 14–43).

[59] Historisk statistik för Sverige. Statistiska översiktstabeller utöver i del I och II publicerade t.o.m. 1950 (1960, p. 99).

[60] Johnson (1985, pp. 89–96 and 110–116). See Wadhwani (2011, pp. 508–509) for the founding of POSB in different countries.

[61] Johnson (1985, p. 205).

in the beginning of the twentieth century.[62] In Sweden, approximately one-third of workers' net savings were deposited in savings banks in the 1870s as well as in the 1900s.[63] Workers were aware of the advantages of having a savings account and could also afford to save. Corresponding results were also shown in a British context.[64]

Prior to the 1870s most account holders in the Swedish savings banks had saved a small amount of their income regularly. Low and uncertain incomes had, however, made long-term savings almost unattainable for most workers and savings accounts, in general, lasted for only a couple of years. Already in the early days of the savings banks, it was common that savers in these banks in Sweden, as well as in several other countries, deposited the maximum amount when the account was opened and used their accounts to safely receive a return on capital.[65] As the rules for deposits at the savings banks' accounts were reformed during the second half of the nineteenth century in Sweden, it became more common that account holders both deposited and withdrew savings several times during the year. Consequently, deposit banking became more multifunctional and flexible in its character than it had previously been. However, few account holders used the bank account in order to save for old age. Instead, from the turn of the twentieth century they often turned to the life assurances that had become popular among the masses.[66] These assurances were built on the principle of collective savings and the guarantee of an agreed amount of money at some time in the future. Savings with the deposit banks were, on the other hand, based on own deposits and only guaranteed the actual saved amount plus interest. An important advantage with deposit banking was, nevertheless, that it was a highly liquid asset.

Saving behaviour as well as the amount saved differed greatly between the socio-economic groups and over the life cycle. At the end of the nineteenth century, wealthier persons often had accounts in commercial banks and savings banks, life insurances, stocks and bonds, all as a

[62] Johnson (1994, p. 122).

[63] Lilja and Bäcklund (2016, p. 127).

[64] Perriton (2012).

[65] Alter et al. (1994, pp. 748–766), Ross (2001, p. 29), Ó Gráda (2003, pp. 38–49) and Lilja (2004, pp. 111–119).

[66] Lilja (2000, pp. 65–69) and Bäcklund and Lilja (2014, p. 632).

strategy to diffuse risks and simultaneously maximize the expected return on equity.[67] For the less-wealthy groups it was, however, seldom possible to save for a long time as investments during different stages of the life cycle had to be paid for. Those who preferred high liquidity and unquestioned security most likely choose a bank account. Collective and contractual saving in sickness and burial funds (friendly societies) and life and endowment funds were, however, probably more prioritized out of family needs.[68]

The changes in the savings banks' charters and the introduction of the savings banks' law of 1892 had been necessary steps for the Swedish savings banks in strengthening their legitimacy as modern deposit banks. They had shown ability to adapt to the transition of Swedish economy during the nineteenth century, and were in 1910 important actors in the deposit market (Table 4.2).

Conclusions and International Comparison

In the 1820s, the Swedish savings banks were role models for the Finnish as well as the Norweigan savings banks' movements. A difference was, however, that a Savings Bank Act was already passed in Norway in 1824, while corresponding laws were first introduced at the end of the nineteenth century in the other Nordic countries. The expansion of the savings banks accelerated in Norway and in the nineteenth century the density of the savings banks net was higher than in the other Nordic countries. On the other hand, the Finnish savings bank expansion was slow, with three urban savings banks by the middle of the nineteenth century. A network of countrywide savings banks was only established at the turn of the twentieth century. The savings banks in Denmark were initially concentrated in the countryside and the capital; however, by the middle of the nineteenth century, urban savings banks became common.[69]

The early Swedish savings banks had been founded out of the ideas that also guided their Scottish and English counterparts, but the early examples of savings funds in the German states were also among their

[67] Lilja (2004, pp. 93–98).

[68] For example, Johnson (1985, pp. 209 and 214–215; 1984, pp. 331–334 and 347), Boyer (2009, pp. 67–72) and Lilja and Bäcklund (2016, pp. 123–126).

[69] Savings Banks Acts were first introduced in Denmark in 1880, Sweden in 1892 and Finland in 1895. Andersen (2011, pp. 80–83, 105–109, 126–128).

predecessors. The latter were often established on the initiative of the municipality, while charity groups in the local society were founders of the savings banks in Great Britain. For example, Russian as well as French savings banks were founded both by public and private interests.[70] Savings banks were market makers for deposit banking not only in Sweden but in several other countries as well.

The strength of their local affiliations was significant for the expansion of Swedish savings banks during the nineteenth century. They had also shown their stability by functioning well without any major mishaps. Savings banks brought trustworthiness to long-term savings. During a period with no direct regulation of the deposit market, transparent and detailed charters were guiding the savings banks in their work. When the size of deposit banking grew and the representatives of the bank could no longer guarantee the business of the bank in person, regulations were introduced to secure account holders' savings. The customers learnt the advantages of saving against compound and a best practice for deposit banking developed over time. By self-adjusting their charters, the Swedish savings banks adapted to new economic conditions and growing competition. As a result, they turned into professionally managed banks at the end of the nineteenth century.

References

Online Sources

Swedish Banking Statistics, SCB (Statistics Sweden).

Unpublished Sources

Nyköping's saving bank (Nyköpings sparbank), Accounting records (Avräkningsböcker), 1832–1862.

Literature

Almén, T. (1930), *Jönköpings stads och läns sparbank 1831–1930*. Jönköping.

[70] Horne (1947, pp. 87–91), Cameron (1967, pp. 106, 165 and 208–210).

Alter, G., Goldin, C., & Rotella, E. (1994), "The Savings of Ordinary Americans: The Philadelphia Saving Fund Society in the Mid-Nineteenth Century". *Journal of Economic History*, Vol. 54, Issue 4, pp. 735–766.

Américi, L. (2002), "Preparing the People for Capitalism: Relations with Depositors in a French Savings Bank During the 1820s". *Financial History Review*, Vol. 9, pp. 5–19.

Andersen, S. E. (2011), *The Evolution of Nordic Finance*. London: Palgrave Macmillan.

Bäcklund, D., & Lilja, K. (2014), "Variation och förnyelse: Arbetarsparandet i Sverige 1870–1914". *Historisk tidskrift*, Vol. 4, pp. 615–646.

Björnstedt, J. (1939), *Sparbanken i Sölvesborg 1839–1939*. Sölvesborg.

Boyer, G. R. (2009), "Insecurity, Safety Nets, and Self-Help in Victorian and Edwardian Britain". In D. Eltis, F. Lewis, & K. L. Sokoloff (Eds.), *Human capital and Institutions: A Long Run View*. Cambridge, MA: Cambridge University Press, pp. 46–89.

Cameron, R. (1967), *Banking in the Early Stages of Development: A Study in Comparative Economic History*. New York: Oxford University Press.

Cronbladh, Å. (1993), "Sparbankerna i Sverige 1820–1992" (Stencil). Stockholm: Institutet för sparbankshistorisk forskning.

Danielsson, H. (1931), *Borås stads sparbank 1831–1931*. Borås.

Fishlow, A. (1961), "The Trustee Savings Banks, 1817–1861". *The Journal of Economic History*, Vol. 21, Issue 1, pp. 26–40.

Haber, C., & Gratton, B. (1993), *Old Age and the Search for Security: An American Social History*. Bloomington & Indianapolis: Indiana University Press.

Historisk statistik för Sverige. Statistiska översiktstabeller utöver i del I och II publicerade t.o.m. 1950 (1960) (*Historical Statistics of Sweden, Statistical Survey. Tables not published in volume I and II*), SCB (Statistical Sweden).

Horne, O. (1947), *A History of Savings Banks*. London/New York/Toronto: Oxford University Press.

Johnson, P. (1984), "Self-Help Versus State Help: Old Age Pensions and Personal Savings in Great Britain, 1906–1937". *Explorations in Economic History*, Vol. 21, pp. 329–350.

Johnson, P. (1985), *Saving and Spending: The Working-Class Economy in Britain 1870–1939*. Oxford: Oxford Historical Monographs.

Johnson, P. (1994), "The Employment and Retirement of Older Men in England and Wales, 1881–1981". *Economic History Review*, Vol. XLVII, Issue 1, pp. 106–128.

Karlsson, M. (2012), *Filantropi under konstruktion: En undersökning av Sällskapet DBW:s samhällsengagemang 1814–1876*. Uppsala: Acta Universitatis Upsaliensis.

Kiesewetter, H. (1981), "Zur Entwicklung sachsischer Sparkassen, zum Sparverhalten und zur Lebenshaltung sachsischer Arbeiter im 19. Jahrhudert (1819–1914)". In W. Conze & U. Engelhardt (Eds.), *Arbeiterexistenz im 19. Jahrhundert*. Stuttgart, pp. 446–486.

Lilja, K. (2000), "Utav omsorg och eftertanke: En undersökning av Falu stads sparbanks sparare 1830–1914". Uppsala Papers in Financial History. No. 11, Uppsala.

Lilja, K. (2004), *Marknad och hushåll: Sparande och krediter i Falun 1820–1910 utifrån ett livscykelperspektiv*. Uppsala: Acta Universitatis Upsaliensis.

Lilja, K. (2010), "The Deposit Market revolution in Sweden". In A. Ögren (Ed.), *The Swedish Financial Revolution*. London: Palgrave MacMillan Studies in Banking and Financial Institutions, pp. 41–63.

Lilja, K., & Bäcklund, D. (2016), "Savings Banks and Working-Class Saving During the Swedish Industrialisation". *Financial History Review*, Vol. 23, Issue 1, pp. 111–132.

Maltby, J. (2011), "The Wife's Administration of the Earnings'?: Working-Class Women and Savings in the Mid-Nineteenth Century". *Continuity and Change*, Vol. 26, pp. 187–217.

Maltby, J., & Rutterford, J. (2006), "'She Possessed Her Own Fortune': Women Investors from the Late Nineteenth Century to the Early Twentieth Century". *Business History*, Vol. 48, Issue 2, pp. 220–253.

Nygren, I. (1981), *Svensk kreditmarknad 1820–1875: Översikt av det institutionella kreditväsendets utveckling*. Göteborg: Meddelanden från ekonomisk-historiska institutionen, Göteborgs universitet.

Nygren, I. (1985), *Från Stockholms Banco till Citibank: Svensk kreditmarknad under 325 år*. Malmö: Liber förlag.

Ó Gráda, C. (2003), "Savings Banks as an Institutional Import: The Case of Nineteenth-Century Ireland". *Financial History Review*, Vol. 10, Issue 1, pp. 31–55.

Ögren, A. (2010), "The Swedish Financial revolution: An In-depth Study". In A. Ögren (Ed.), *The Swedish Financial revolution*. London: Palgrave MacMillan Studies in Banking and Financial Institutions, pp. 1–13.

Olmstead, A. L. (1975), "Mutual Savings Bank Depositors in New York". *Business History Review*, Vol. XLIX, Issue 3 (autumn), pp. 287–311.

Owens, A. (2006), "'Making Some Provision for the Contingencies to Which Their Sex Is Particular Liable': Women and Investment in Early Nineteenth Century ENGLAND". In R. Beachy, B. Craig, & A. Owens (Eds.), *Rethinking Separate Spheres. Women, Business and Finance in Nineteenth-Century Europe*. London & New York: Berg Publishers, pp. 20–35.

Payne, P. L. (1967), "The Savings Bank of Glasgow 1836–1914". In P. L. Payne (Ed.), *Studies in Scottish Business History*. London, pp. 152–186.

Perlinge, A. (2005), *Sockenbankirerna: Kreditrelationer och tidig bankverksamhet. Vånga socken i Skåne 1840–1900*. Stockholm: Nordiska museets förlag.

Perriton, L. (2012), "Depositor Trends in the Limehouse Savings Bank". *Worlds Savings Banks Institute/European Savings Banks Groups.*

Perriton, L., & Maltby, J. (2015), "Working-Class Households and Savings in England, 1850–1880". *Enterprise & Society*, Vol. 16, pp. 413–445.

Petersson, T. (2001), *Framväxten av ett lokalt banksystem: Oppunda sparbank, Södermanlands enskilda bank och stationssamhället Katrineholm 1850–1916.* Uppsala: Acta Universitatis Upsaliensis.

Petersson, T. (2006), "The Silent Partners: Women, Capital and the Development of the Financial System in Nineteenth-Century Sweden". In R. Beachy, B. Craig, & A. Owens (Eds.), *Rethinking Separate Spheres. Women, Business and Finance in Nineteenth-century Europe*. London & New York: Berg Publishers, pp. 36–51.

Ross, D. M. (2001), "Between Philanthropy and Entrepreneurship: Two Scottish Savings Banks in the Early Nineteenth Century". In M. Henrekson, M. Larsson, & H. Sjögren (Eds.), *Entrepreneurship in Business and Research: Essays in Honour of Håkan Lindgren*. Stockholm: Institute for Research in Economic History, Stockholm School of Economics, pp. 301–326.

Ross, D. M. (2013), "Savings Banks Depositors in a Crisis, Glasgow in 1847 and 1857". *Financial History Review*, Vol. 20, pp. 183–208.

Samuelsson, K. (1978), *Postbanken—postsparbank och postgiro 1884–1925–1974.* Stockholm: Postverket.

Schulz, G. (1981), "Der konnte freilich ganz anders sparen als ich". In W. Conze & U. Engelhardt (Eds.), *Arbeiterexistenz in 19. Jahrhundert: Lebensstandard un Lebensgestaltung deutscher Arbeiter und Handwerker*. Stuttgart, pp. 487–515.

Silow, A. (1926), *Falu stads sparbank 1825–1925*. Falun.

Sjölander, A. (2003), *Den naturliga ordningen: Makt och intressen i de svenska sparbankerna 1882–1968*. Uppsala: Acta Universitatis Upsaliensis.

Skogman, C.-D. (1819), *Underrättelse om så kallade besparingsbanker*. Stockholm.

Sommarin, E. (1940), *Grundläggningen av vårt sparbanksväsen*. Stockholm.

Sommarin, E. (1942), *Vårt sparbanksväsen 1834–1892*. Lund.

Underdånigt betänkande angående Sveriges ekonomiska och finansiella utveckling under åren 1834–1860 (1863). (1858 års Finanskommitté III). Stockholm.

Varifrån kommer, hur uppstår sparkapitalet? (1946), Unpublished manuscript regarding Stockholms savings bank.

Wadhwani, R. D. (2002), "Banking from the Bottom Up: The Case of Migrant Savers at the Philadelphia Saving Fund Society During the Late Nineteenth Century". *Financial History Review*, Vol. 9, pp. 41–63.

Wadhwani, R. D. (2011), "The Institutional Foundations of Personal Finance: Innovation in U.S. Savings Banks, 1880s–1920s". *Business History Review*, Vol. 85, pp. 499–528.

CHAPTER 5

Credit Risks: From Networks and Cooperation to Stable Markets

Abstract This chapter focusses on how local savings banks invested the deposits and how they dealt with the risks connected to such activities. To a large extent, especially in the first phases of their development, the managers of savings banks had to rely on their personal and social network in order to minimize risk. In later stages, as the savings banks had built up their own financial competence, and as formal regulations regarding investments were introduced, granting credit and loans became more standardized processes and allowed the saving banks to compete with especially the commercial banks.

Keywords Social networks · Cooperation · Insider lending · Competition · Standardization

Introduction

From the early 1820s, a vast majority of the Swedish savings banks were focussed on investing a lion part of their deposits on the local credit markets. Lending to local industry, commerce and agriculture became a hallmark of the early Swedish savings banks. This very intentional but at the same time pragmatic investment policy forms an apparent

M. Larsson et al., *Risk Management in Early Banking*, Palgrave Studies in the History of Finance, https://doi.org/10.1007/978-3-030-80775-7_5

contrast between the Swedish savings banks on one hand and many of the savings banks in other Western European countries on the other. The early nineteenth-century savings banks in for example Denmark, England, Scotland, France and Belgium did not in general have any active investment policies at all. The type of assets the savings banks in these countries could hold was closely circumscribed by legislation, and they did not invest in, or lend to, local or regional industry or business at all. Instead, the savings banks' investments were highly concentrated on government bonds.[1] However, analogues to the Swedish case of active, local investment policies did exist. The most obvious case is the Norwegian savings banks but also savings banks in Germany, Austria and Hungary were to some extent showing the same pattern of adaptation to local credit demands and a high degree of independence from governmental regulation.[2]

In the late nineteenth century, from the 1870s, a distinct shift in the investments and lending operations of the Swedish savings banks took place. It was both a quantitative and qualitative change and had far-reaching consequences, especially on the lending activities of both individual savings and on the savings banks in general. Previous investment and lending policies, which had been adapted to local, and even individual, preconditions and credit demands, were now step-by-step abandoned in favour of more standardized and predictable practices. By introducing the idea of "the natural order" on the Swedish credit market the State set up institutional boundaries of what the different financial organizations were to do, and consequently, *not* to do. Regarding the savings banks and their investment and lending activities, they were instructed, or at least strongly advised, to concentrate their investments to fully securefully secure alternatives, such as mortgages and state bonds, and thus to avoid lending to industrial and commercial purposes. These kinds of investments and lending, being more risky, but at the same time very profitable, were to be the prime objective of the rapidly expanding private commercial banks.[3]

[1] Horne (1947), Cameron (1967), Born (1983), Collins (1991), Hollis and Sweetman (1998), Américi (2002), Ross (2002) and Ó Gráda (2003).

[2] Thomes (1995), Edwards and Ogilvie (1996) and Tomka (2002).

[3] Sjölander (2003).

Concerning the growth of the entire institutional credit market one must recognize the vast quantitative increase taking place from the late 1860s and on. The total volume of the Swedish institutional credit approximately redoubled every tenth year up to the early twentieth century. Credits from the rather newly established financial organizations, such as the savings banks but even more so from the commercial banks and the mortgage institutions, thus replaced those credits previously handled by the non-institutional, or informal, credit market actors, such as merchant houses, local dealers and brokers. Several comprehensive empirical studies made on the ratio between the non-institutionalized and the institutionalized credit systems in Sweden, and some less extensive studies on the Danish and Norwegian markets, has shown that the earlier, pre-industrial credit system actually was in good health all the way up to the turn of the nineteenth century.

In the mid-nineteenth century, up to 80–90 per cent of the total credit volume on local credit markets consisted of credits granted by non-institutional lenders, such as relatives, friends and other private local moneylenders. Still as late as 1900, when we had dense networks of banks and other financial intermediaries, up to 40 per cent of total credits were handled on the informal credit market. Trust between individuals, i.e. *personal trust*, and social control was only gradually replaced by trust in institutions, formal regulations and standardization, i.e. *system trust*. Later in this chapter, we will highlight the role of savings banks in the transition from informal to formal credit markets.[4] In analyzing the role of the savings banks on the domestic credit market one must bear in mind that the quantitative shift in the 1860s and 1870s was apparently simultaneous to a qualitative shift in the investment and lending operations of the savings banks. In other words, when the institutional credit market switched into the road to speedy growth, the savings banks in many cases were more or less hindered by the institutional set up to engage in credit transactions that previously had been a natural part of their operations.

[4] Several estimations have been done on the Swedish case, see Lindgren (2002), Hellgren (2003, pp. 61–88), Lilja (2004, pp. 129–148) and Perlinge (2005, pp. 264–267). See also estimations on other Scandinavian countries in Hansen (1982, p. 580), Skånland (1967, p. 74) and Brandal et al. (1989, pp. 22–23).

This chapter deals with the investments and lending operations of the Swedish savings banks. It is divided into two, chronological parts; the first one starts in the 1820s, thus embracing the initial, formative phase of the Swedish savings banks, and ends in 1870. During the second time period in this chapter, 1870–1910, the managers, staff and directors of the savings banks faced somewhat different problems regarding how to manage the risks involved in carrying through investments and lending.

The savings banks were in the last decades of the nineteenth century not only considered being well established, sustainable and perpetual financial organizations by the general public, but the expectations and demands, especially those one stemming from the State, and its local and regional governmental bodies, on what the savings banks *should* do had somewhat altered. One of their primary missions was now to engage both in large-scale financing of the urbanization process, i.e. foremost the financing of modern dwellings, and at the same time to offer a fully secure investment choice to the public. "Avoid risk" and "support the local industrialisation process" was the motto for the savings banks, a motto set up by the State.

Notwithstanding the division of this chapter into two parts, and even though the fact that the savings banks had to deal with rather different problems in the latter period than in the first, some common issues will be addressed in both parts of the chapter;

- The structures of the investments—what was the quantitative relation between the savings banks and other major financial organizations on the Swedish institutional credit market, and how and why did it change over time?
- Risk profile and risk management—how did the savings banks choose to transform the deposits into prolific investments, i.e. how did they allocate the deposits into the different available investment opportunities, which in turn had different degrees of risks?
- The borrowers and the role as financiers—to whom did the savings banks choose to lend, and what role did savings banks have in the larger societal processes of industrialization and urbanization of the Swedish economy?

Personal Networks, Cooperation and Insider Lending, 1820–1870

The founding fathers and the first generation of managers in the Swedish savings banks faced some principal, and probably rather challenging, problems to overcome, *if* the savings banks were to survive and become the long-term intermediaries they've proven to be in a handful of other European countries. The question of legitimacy and trust, and the importance of the founding fathers' societal status in the local communities for the successful establishment and development of the Swedish savings banks, has been addressed in Chapter 3.

A somewhat more tangible issue was how to deal with the uncertainties connected to making loans to the public since a vast majority of the newly established Swedish savings banks gradually engaged in such activities. Considering the investment alternatives for the early nineteenth-century savings banks, it must be noted that they in fact were not so many. The issuing of bonds, both private and government bonds, were at a minimal level in the first half the century. Not surprisingly, the breakthrough of the Swedish bond market coincided with the general revolution of the domestic financial markets, i.e. the late 1860s and the 1870s.[5]

Despite the fact that the national government supported the idea of savings banks being established in as many locations as possible, they were not willing to, or actually did not have the financial means to, directly support the savings banks. Hence, the Swedish government ***did not*** offer the savings banks a secure investment alternative for the depositors' money, as governments in some other European countries did. The local savings banks then had to find other ways to invest and other ways to make their banks viable in the long-term.

The two remaining principal investment alternatives left to choose between for the early savings banks was thus either to reinvest the deposits with other, already prevalent intermediaries on the local financial markets, or to start engaging themselves in lending operations. The first alternative, to hope that local businessmen, trading houses, etc. would be willing to receive the money from the savings banks' depositors, on a regular basis and at foreseeable and long-term conditions, was both rather risky and in some cases, not even a conceivable alternative, simply due to the fact of a lack of such (willing) intermediaries.

[5] Petersson (2001, p. 147).

The second alternative—to engage in lending operations—was thus in fact more or less the only possible investment alternative left to the early Swedish savings banks. Consequently, the savings banks, just as any bank regardless of time and space, faced the fundamental problem of asymmetric information. Since borrower default is an ever-existing uncertainty in bank lending, minimizing this asymmetric information on borrowers and their short- and long-term creditworthiness is essential to avoid such default. But before we get into how the early Swedish savings banks solved the problem of asymmetric information and the risks connected to giving loans, we shall examine how the total institutional credit market in Sweden developed up to 1870.

When this process was illustrated (Table 5.1), it was obvious that the savings banks developed into, if not an immediate success, at least one important intermediator on the domestic credit market. With about 15 per cent of the total credit volume, the savings banks were the third most important category of credit intermediators on the aggregate Swedish credit market by the year of 1870, surpassed by the mortgage organizations and the commercial banks.

Getting deeper into the structure of the savings banks' investments, the focus on giving loans becomes much apparent. Statistics are not available for the first three decades addressed in this chapter (1820–1840s), but from the year 1850 and on we do know that more than 80 per cent of

Table 5.1 The Swedish institutional credit market 1835–1870, shares in per cent

Year	*Savings banks*	*Commercial banks*	*Mortgage organizations*	*The National Bank of Sweden*	*Others*
1835	6	6	6	82	0
1840	8	16	21	49	6
1845	8	13	24	46	9
1850	11	16	33	35	5
1855	13	16	46	22	3
1860	12	24	38	18	8
1865	12	25	43	12	8
1870	14	29	38	10	9

Source Nygren (1983, pp. 37 and 49)

all deposits in the Swedish savings banks were transformed into loans to the public. In 1850 85 per cent of all deposits were transformed into loans, in 1860 the quota had risen to 93 per cent and in 1870 it was still as high as 92 per cent. In comparison with the commercial banks this quota was high. The commercial banks had yet, i.e. around the mid of the nineteenth century, not more than 50–60 per cent of their investments placed in loans to the public.[6]

Disregarding whether the concentration on giving loans reflected an intentional desire on the behalf of the founding fathers and the first generation of managers to develop the savings banks into long-term intermediators on the local credit markets, or, if it was a decision made by necessity, it is obvious that the Swedish savings banks in this stage of development responded to a demand for credits as well as for other financial services on numerous local markets.

Returning then to the question of how the problem of asymmetric information was solved, the early savings banks surely did not have the resources necessary to monitor the borrowers, as the underlying theoretical argumentation suggests. Since the savings banks based their operations on a minimum of external capital, in fact on the paid-in capital of the founding fathers and furthermore depending entirely on voluntary efforts by the same individuals, they had not in the initial stages saved up the necessary financial resources to carry through such monitoring of the borrowers. The two remaining alternatives were then (1) extensive use of insider lending and/or, (2) cooperation with other financial intermediaries, especially with the commercial banks, in order to get access to vital resources such as information on debtors and in some cases, to create risk sharing among the creditors.

The use of insider lending, i.e. the providing of loans from the bank to the banks' managers, owners and their associates, in the early stages of a financial intermediary's development has by previous research been interpreted as an effective way of lowering the risks connected with giving loans. But at the same time, from the borrowers' point of view, insider lending was a way of getting access to credits on reasonable conditions.[7] Considering the traditions and characteristics of that day Swedish financial system, insider lending was indeed widely spread among all categories of

[6] Petersson (2001, p. 75).

[7] Lamoreaux (1986, 1991, 1994).

financial intermediaries, from the smallest rural savings bank to the large, internationally oriented commercial bank. Furthermore, it was a generally accepted way of doing banking business, at least up to the Second World War. Instead of considering the extensive practice of insider loans among the Swedish banks as signs of hazardous preferential treatment, potentially threatening the well-being of the bank and the interests of their share-/stakeholders, the insider loans were by and large understood as signs of in deep trust between the bank, its managers, owners, and customers.

Hence, the use of insider loans was not surprisingly widespread among the savings banks. In the historical monographs of several early savings banks such loans were motivated by an urgent need for somewhere to place the first deposits, at acceptable interest rates. Taking an example of exactly how widespread the phenomenon of insider lending was, the results from a study on one of the early urban savings banks could be used. The savings bank in the town of Nyköping, a middle-sized town about 80 kms south of Stockholm, was founded in 1832 and was in several aspects a typical exponent of the early Swedish savings banks.

To the core group of founding fathers and first generation of managers belonged to the upper layers of the local and regional society, i.e. merchants and manufacturers, the landed gentry and, of course, the county governor. The board of directors was consequently dominated by the same socio-economical categories during the entire nineteenth century. The savings bank in Nyköping was as most of its counterparts throughout Sweden, almost entirely focussed on giving loans to the public. Between 87 and 100 per cent of the collected deposits were transformed into loans from the establishment of the bank up to 1870.[8]

Insider lending occurred from the very beginning in the savings bank in Nyköping. Initially, up to the late 1830s, the two dominating founding fathers—the brothers Pehr and Abraham Löfvenius and their trading company—borrowed the majority of the deposits in the savings banks. Insiders in the savings bank did not only grant loans to themselves, relatives, and business associates, they also made personal guarantees for borrowers that were "outsiders". In some years more than 80 per cent of annual lending can be categorized as insider lending. In 1846, however, the accountants of the savings banks protested against the level of insider lending. The accountants also suggested a maximum amount that one

[8] Petersson (2000).

single person could be responsible for—both as a borrower and as a guarantor. The board of directors however rejected the suggestion with the motive that the board at all times thoroughly assessed the quality of offered collateral. The insider loans thus continued to be a hallmark of the lending operations, and never fell below 50 per cent of total lending, and in some years reaching over 90 per cent.[9]

Turning then to the question of cooperation with other financial intermediaries, and how such cooperation influenced the investments and lending operations of savings banks, the cooperation with local and regional commercial banks was the most widespread throughout the country. One reason to the extensive cooperation between savings banks and commercial banks in Sweden was the fact that the savings banks in many cases were market makers on the local credit *and* deposit markets. In the year 1850, 42 out of 43 cities that had a commercial bank or a branch office of a commercial bank, a savings bank had been established prior to the commercial bank. Furthermore, when the commercial bank was established it was generally the same founding fathers in both categories of banks. The prerequisites for in deep cooperation were thus based on personal knowledge and of common interests.[10]

One consequence of the close personal relations between savings banks and commercial banks were that the savings banks often got a somewhat subordinate role in relation to the commercial bank. Large loans, as well as large deposits, were in many cases directed to the commercial banks, with reference to the fact that the savings banks should not, and could not, get engaged in large-scale and risky lending. The bank-industry networks that from the late nineteenth century was such a distinct feature of the Swedish banking system, was yet in an embryonic stage. However, it was obvious already in first half of the century that the savings banks did play, and probably would continue to play, a subordinate and assisting role in the establishment and development of these networks.

Taking the savings bank in Nyköping again as an example of how the actual lending operations looked like in the early savings banks, an example that is supported by studies of the savings banks in Gothenburg, reveals that local businessmen, industry and commerce in general made up the bulk of the borrowers in the savings bank (Table 5.2). Both small-scale

[9] Petersson (2000).

[10] Petersson (2001, p. 88).

Table 5.2 The loans given by the savings bank in Nyköping 1835–1870, shares of total lending, in per cent

Year	*Agri-culture*	*Landed gentry and higher officers*	*Shop-keepers and whole-sale dealers*	*Manu-facturers and crafts-men*	*Public officials*	*Local autho-rities*	*Others*
1835	5	34	23	26	0	0	12
1840	11	25	20	26	8	0	10
1845	20	14	12	22	12	0	20
1850	21	22	3	25	9	0	20
1855	20	19	12	17	16	2	14
1860	12	27	10	11	16	2	22
1865	12	22	7	13	10	15	21
1870	18	22	8	13	6	14	19

Source Petersson (2000)

merchants and larger industrial companies used the local savings bank to finance short- and long-term investments. This frequent pattern of industrial and commercial financing stands out as a feature of the early Swedish savings banks.[11]

To sum up the first period, i.e. 1820–1870, the investments and lending operations of the Swedish savings banks in general shows some distinct characteristics, albeit one must take into account that there is a lack of all-embracing statistical sources. There are however numerous examples of how local savings banks throughout Sweden from the early nineteenth century and on, adopted a wide set of financial activities in order to support local commerce and industry. Some savings banks, especially the ones situated in the larger cities, were thus more or less entirely focussed on granting loans to industry and local businesses in general when it came to making decisions on how to invest the incoming deposits. The rural savings banks were naturally, as their Nordic counterparts, also designated to invest in loans to local and regional agriculture.[12]

[11] Petersson (2000), and Nygren (1987).

[12] Nygren (1967), Petersson (2000; 2001, pp. 76–79 and 200–203).

Table 5.3 The investment structure of the Swedish savings banks 1880–1910, in per cent of total investments

Year	*Lending*	*Bonds*	*Deposits in other banks*	*Other*	*Total assets, in millions SEK at constant prices [1880]*
1880	77	17	5	1	158
1890	79	12	5	4	276
1900	79	12	4	5	469
1910	82	10	4	4	940

Source Petersson (2001, p. 75)

Detailed studies of the structure of the borrowers in the savings banks have furthermore revealed a clear, but, however, not surprising, discrepancy between the socio-economic background of the depositors and the borrowers, respectively. For example, female borrowers were (of course) very rare, despite the fact that they made up the backbone of the depositors. The typical borrower in the Swedish savings banks was thus a male, in his most active years (30–50 years), engaged in locally based business activity and belonging to the middle- or higher socio-economic classes of society.[13]

Market Stabilization, Standardization and "The Natural Order", 1870–1910

The Swedish savings banks continued to concentrate their investments into giving loans to the public all the way up to the early twentieth century. The domestic market for issuing bonds did grow at a fast rate, giving the savings banks alternatives to invest in both private and public bonds. However, a majority of the savings banks chose to stick to their traditions of giving loans, instead of investing in bonds (Table 5.3).

The time period from the 1820s to 1870 was characterized by efforts to establish and develop the savings banks on the emerging institutional credit markets. Other fundamental issues now gradually replaced the principal problems that had to be addressed in the initial period. Without a

[13] Hellgren (2003, pp. 113–133), Lilja (2004, pp. 142–146), and Perlinge (2005, pp. 192–193).

doubt the founding fathers and first generation of managers had been able to create trust in the new savings banks among the general public and the savings banks were at this stage considered as well established and trustworthy financial organizations.

The savings banks now had to turn their focus on, firstly, how to in an efficient and viable way deal with the increasing number of loans and credit volumes and, secondly, how to continue to successfully compete with other financial intermediaries, especially because the number of commercial banks and branch offices increased at a fast rate. The commercial banks also turned their attention to the traditional customer groups in the savings banks, both on the deposit and the credit side.

Two simultaneous processes thus appeared, the first being the *professionalization* of savings banks' organizations, and especially on the management level, and the second being a *standardization* of the financial services offered by the savings banks.

The growth of business in many savings banks demanded more active governance. Donors and management were gradually separated, and the important social and legitimacy-bringing role of the founding fathers had by and large been played out. Fulltime managers and staff were hired to fulfil the tasks previously carried out on a voluntary, and unpaid, basis. At the end of the nineteenth century most Swedish savings banks, with the exception of the smallest—often rural—savings banks, had full-time managers and other personnel working for them.

The second, necessary process was the one of standardizing the financial services offered, and this process was naturally interconnected to the one of professionalization. Many savings banks now handled hundreds of loan applications every year. Earlier, when the lending operations generally were on a smaller scale, the savings banks could make use of individual social control of the borrowers. If you were to get a loan in the local savings bank, you had to get the approval of your personal character besides proving your creditworthiness of course. In the later stages such a control mechanism, based on personal knowledge and social control, was not possible to uphold (see also Chapter 6).

The transaction costs would simply have been too large. The credit contracts were then from the 1870s considerably standardized in order to meet these demands. Consequently, there was a qualitative shift in the structure of collaterals. Another factor behind the shift towards mortgage as the dominating form of collateral was change in the institutional set up. In 1875 changes in the laws concerning mortgages and the legal

Table 5.4 Collateral in the lending of the Swedish savings banks 1876–1910, shares in per cent

Year	*Mortgage*	*Name*	*Shares*	*Total advances, in millions SEK*
1876	51	44	5	116
1880	56	40	4	121
1890	64	31	5	241
1900	68	24	8	362
1910	71	21	8	693

Source Petersson (2001, p. 78)

ratification of properties made it considerably easier, and cheaper, than before to give loans on mortgage.[14] Personal guarantee had been the dominating form of collateral in the early stages, but now became less and less apparent. In the early twentieth century around 20 per cent of the collateral was personal guarantee (Table 5.4).

The general development of the savings banks' investments and role on the total Swedish credit market in quantitative terms is one characterized by stability and indicates that the savings banks actually were able to adapt to the new conditions, and the hardened competition, on the domestic credit market in the late nineteenth century. The savings banks thus continued to have between 15 and 20 per cent of the total Swedish credit market (Table 5.5). The credit organizations that can be characterized as "winners", were definitely the commercial banks. They were very successful in attracting borrowers, especially from the fast growing industrial, and often export-oriented companies. The mortgage institutions as a contrast lost considerable market shares, due to the agricultural sectors' need for credits gradually diminished towards the end of the century.

What changes can we then observe concerning the borrowers in the savings banks? Firstly, we must again take in an important institutional change, i.e. the introduction of "the natural order". With the introduction of the Savings Banks Act of 1892, the government stated that the savings banks' "natural line of business" was one that included risk-minimizing investment strategies. Savings banks were to invest only in fully secure alternatives, such as mortgages, and *not* compete with the

[14] Petersson (2001, pp. 76–77).

Table 5.5 The Swedish formal credit market 1875–1910, shares in per cent

Year	*Savings banks*	*Commercial banks*	*Mortgage organizations*	*The National Bank of Sweden*	*Others*
1875	16	38	30	7	9
1880	14	35	35	8	8
1885	17	38	30	7	8
1890	19	36	29	7	9
1895	21	40	24	6	9
1900	18	50	17	6	9
1905	19	52	13	7	9
1910	19	54	13	5	9

Source Nygren (1983, pp. 49 and 60; 1985, p. 150)

commercial banks in lending to industry and other commercial activities considered to be risky and potentially hazardous. As described above, many local savings banks had for many years devoted a large portion of their investments to loans to local business, industry and commerce. Hence, with the introduction of "the natural order" many savings banks were disqualified from continuing to perform banking business, such as short-term lending to local industry and the offering of financial services such as accounting of bills, i.e. services that too much resembled those performed by the continuously growing number of commercial banks. The new legislation was officially motivated by concerns of the well-being of the depositors, the savings banks should not be given the possibility to risk the savings of "ordinary" people, but apparently also had some effects on the savings banks ability to compete on the local credit markets.[15]

Some savings banks did continue to engage in the financing of business and industry even after the institutional change, especially in the newly industrialized cities in the north of Sweden, but the general trend was still a change towards more long-term and delimited lending operations. As the shift in collateral suggests (Table 5.4), mortgages gradually become the hallmark of lending of the Swedish savings banks, a hallmark that persisted for the entire twentieth century. Considering the external financing of houses, the savings bank had a market share of 25 per cent

[15] Sjölander (2003).

(of the total volume of external credits for housing mortgages), in the early 1910s.[16]

Case studies of local savings banks throughout Sweden confirm the general picture described above. The number of loans granted by the savings banks increased sharply from the 1870s, reflecting the fact that it was now possible for new, large categories of borrowers to get loans in savings banks. The industrial revolution and its obvious consequences, such as the increasing urbanization and the need for new and better living conditions in the cities, naturally had a great impact on this process. The standardized contracts in the savings banks and the new forms of collateral used by a majority of the savings banks gradually gave the savings banks a distinct character of being a bank for the growing working class. When the own-your-own-home associations had their breakthrough in the early twentieth century, this character became all the more noticeable as these associations to a large degree depended on credits from the local savings banks.[17]

Returning again to the question of cooperation with the commercial banks and the savings banks' role in the local and regional bank-industry networks, it becomes even more apparent than earlier that the savings banks were to be subordinate and supportive in relation to the commercial banks. An example of the logic and actual functioning of such a local and regional bank-industry network can be taken from the railway junction community of Katrineholm, a typical exponent of the Swedish industrial revolution in the late nineteenth century. Katrineholm was established when the nationwide railway system was being built from the 1850s and on. It immediately attracted both people, businesses, and capital. In a couple of decades Katrineholm had become a regional centre of commerce, industry, and population.

In 1881 a savings bank, Oppunda savings bank (originally established as a parish savings bank in 1850) moved its head office to the expanding community of Katrineholm. The following year a regional commercial bank, Södermanlands enskilda bank, also established their business in Katrineholm. Cooperation between the two banks emerged immediately. For instance, the savings banks acted as exchange representatives for the commercial bank, and it also on several occasions passed on

[16] Bergström (1916, pp. 178–179).

[17] Fälting (2001).

credits that were too large for them to handle to Södermanlands enskilda bank. Not surprisingly, the number of interlocking directorates and joint office holders between the savings bank and the commercial bank grew steadily over time, thus permitting information on potential customers' creditworthiness to flow freely within this personal network.

The most dominant feature of the banking system that emerged in the community of Katrineholm was however the large concentration of loans to local industry and commerce, or in other words; the emergence of a local bank-industry network. These loans were to a large extent cases of insider lending, i.e. the borrowers at the same held key positions in the banks that granted the loans. A small group of individuals controlled not only the two banks and a number of businesses within commerce and industry. They also had a large influence in the local governmental bodies. The close personal ties between the savings bank and the commercial bank—including the founding fathers of the savings bank, the owners of the commercial bank, the boards and the managements of the savings bank and the commercial bank respectively—is a reason why the savings bank seemed to have been the loosing part of this equation. There was, at least in some cases, a clear tendency to transfer the most profitable businesses, and clients, *from* the savings bank *to* the commercial bank, as these could be used directly to increase the individual wealth of its managers and/or owners.[18]

But if we disregard such more or less moralistic interpretations of the implications of the personal relations between savings banks and commercial banks, it is obvious that the Swedish savings banks continued to play an active role in the development of local credit markets also from the early twentieth century and on. The most important mission accomplished was probably solving the problem of financing the housing of the working class and the continued mechanization and general modernization of small-scale farms. By reorganizing their day-to-day operations and by introducing standard lending practices on a large scale the savings banks could handle much larger volumes of loans and customers. The professionalization of the organization and new, better and less costly ways of treating the risks associated to giving loans, were important explanations to why the Swedish savings were able to reorganize themselves and adapt to new market conditions in the nineteenth century.

[18] Petersson (2001); Chapter 7 in this volume. Other, similar examples in Nygren (1967, 1970a, b, 1987).

It is also important to recognize the crucial role of savings banks in bridging the gap between the pre-modern, informal credit system based on personal trust and social control and the new, more institutionalized, regulated and formalized credit system, based on system trust and widely accepted standards. In an extensive study of both borrowers and lenders in the town of Sala between 1860 and 1910, the transition of the local credit system—from informal to formal—is studied in detail. The town of Sala was a major Swedish mining town since the sixteenth century, producing silver for coinage, and a regional commercial and industrial centre. The Sala savings bank was established in 1831 and was until the 1860s the only bank in town, as two commercial banks established branch offices there.[19]

The lending practices of Sala savings bank depended heavily on personal collateral or guarantee loans. The borrowers had to submit at least two, sometimes three, guarantors that assured the repayment of the loan. If the borrower failed to fulfil his obligations, the savings bank could turn to the guarantors for repayment. The guarantors then, were in many cases guarantors for several loans, not only in the savings bank but also on the informal credit market. And, which reveals mutually beneficent character of this local system, many of the borrowers were simultaneously also guarantors themselves. As a result, borrowers, guarantors, and the savings bank, were intertwined into an intrinsic system of personal relations and social control which the common goal of increasing trust and decreasing individual and organizational risk. Apparently, this system worked. The Sala savings bank suffered virtually no credit losses at all. Eventually, after the turn of the nineteenth century, the lending policies and practices of Sala savings banks changed, towards increased use of mortgages. But, which is the main point, by accepting the procedures and practices of the pre-modern credit system, the Sala savings banks contributed in making the transition process to the modern credit system more continuous and more inclusive for the traditional segments of customers in the bank.

[19] Hellgren (2003).

Conclusions and International Comparisons

This chapter has focussed on the investments and the lending operations of the Swedish savings banks, from the establishment of the first savings banks in the 1820s to the early twentieth century. During this period, the Swedish economy underwent a dramatic development that transformed the country from a relatively poor agricultural economy to an industrialized one. Sweden, as well as the other Nordic countries, thus developed from being comparatively backward in all economic aspects to an economy characterized by general growth and prosperity. The industrial revolution was accompanied by a financial revolution, consisting by instance of a rapid growth in the number of financial organizations, of financial services offered to a greater public and of a general quantitative and qualitative shift in these services. And the savings banks, their investments and loans to the public were an essential part of the Swedish financial revolution.

The principal question addressed in this chapter has been how and by which means the savings banks solved the problem of risk connected to performing financial investments and especially to giving loans to the public. The question of risk management had to be solved during quite different and changing external circumstances throughout the period studied, taking into consideration not only the general conditions, such as demand and supply of credits, on local and regional markets but also the impact of government regulations and furthermore also the actions of competitors.

The more quantitative development of the investments and lending operations of the Swedish savings banks is rather straightforward and uncomplicated. The savings banks from the very beginning devoted a vast majority of their investments to loans to the public. In general, between 70 and 80 per cent of the total investments made by the savings banks consisted of loans to the public. Consequently, the savings banks developed into a major player on the total domestic credit market. In the early twentieth century the savings banks had a market share of nearly 20 per cent of the total credit market.

Turning to the more qualitative development, especially considering the lending operations, we can identify rather different hallmarks during the early development phase (1820–1870) on one hand and the latter phase (1870–1910) on the other. The early phase was characterized by networks, by cooperation with other financial organizations and by insider lending. The founding fathers of the savings banks and the first generation of managers thus made extensive use of their personal networks and relations in taking investment decisions in "their" savings banks. The savings banks were in many cases the first institutionalized financial intermediator to be established on the local credit market, thus to some extent replacing, or at least complementing, more informal sources of credits such as local merchants and money brokers. Since the savings banks also lacked the necessary resources to build up an organization to systematically control and supervise a large group of borrowers' alternative ways of minimizing the financial risks connected to lending had to be found. Using personal relations to point out credit- and trustworthy borrowers and to make use of more informal, or social, control of the borrowers was thus the method used by many of the early savings banks. Insider lending was then consequently a rather widespread phenomenon among these savings banks. This might have reduced the banks risk, but did not necessary increase legitimacy and trust.

Somewhere around 1870 we can identify a qualitative shift in the investments and lending operations of the savings banks. Firstly, the use of mortgages as collateral had its breakthrough, thus replacing personal guarantee as the dominant form of collateral. This shift was partly due to the fact that many savings banks had developed into rather large financial intermediaries and simply couldn't handle the growing numbers of borrowers. The use of personal guarantee as collateral demanded personal knowledge of the borrowers on the behalf of the savings bank, its organization and its managers and personnel. If a savings bank had a large number of borrowers and hundreds, or maybe even thousands of loan applications every year it was not any longer possible to uphold a system based on personal knowledge. The shift towards mortgage as the dominant form of collateral was furthermore spurred by an institutional change, making it much less complicated and less time-consuming to use mortgages as collateral. To sum up the circumstances surrounding this specific change, the transaction costs to give loans on mortgage, in relation to using personal guarantee, was considerably lowered.

We can also distinguish a rather apparent change in the characteristics of the typical borrower in the savings banks. In the early stages loans to local business, commerce and industry had dominated in many savings banks, both in rural and urban areas. In the late nineteenth century the urban savings banks by and large devoted their lending operations to the increasing demand for financing of housing for the growing working classes. In the rural areas on the other hand, the importance of the savings banks was clearly their effort to meet the credit demands from small-scale farmers. In all, the changing character of the lending operations during the late nineteenth century and the early twentieth century established the savings banks as being a bank for the lower and middle classes, i.e. a bank for "ordinary people". This character has then been very apparent during the bulk of the twentieth century.

An important part of how risk management was conducted in individual savings banks was their role in the local and regional bank-industry networks that appeared from the mid-nineteenth century throughout the country. The savings banks had an important function of being market makers on the local financial markets and acquired valuable knowledge, information, and practical experiences from these markets. When cooperating with other, later established financial organizations, especially the commercial banks, these capabilities in many cases were used to build up local and regional bank-industry networks. The role of the savings banks in these networks was clearly a complementary one, supporting the long-term development of both commercial banks and the industrial and commercial interests within the networks. The savings banks thus took care of the less risky, and less profitable, financial operations conducted by the financial organizations within the networks.

How can we then characterize the investments and lending operations of the Swedish savings banks in an international, comparative perspective? In the *Nordic* context the Norwegian savings banks stands out as the most successful ones (Table 5.6). In the early twentieth century the Norwegian savings banks had a market share of almost one third of the domestic credit market. The savings banks in Norway had a stronger local and independent character than for example the Swedish savings banks, which also in many cases prevented commercial banks from establishing on local and regional financial markets for a long time. Hence, the Norwegian savings banks did not accept to take on a subordinate role in relation to commercial banks as the Swedish savings often did. The Norwegian savings banks were thus the most successful of the Nordic savings banks in offering vital and long-term assistance to the developments of local and regional industry, commerce, and municipal infrastructure and also to the general economic development.[20]

[20] Egge (1983), Brandal et al. (1989) and Thue (2014).

Table 5.6 Market-shares on the institutional credit markets in the Scandinavian countries, 1840–1910. Savings banks (SB), commercial banks (CB) and national banks (NB), per cent

Year	*Denmark*			*Finland*			*Norway*			*Sweden*		
	SB	*CB*	*NB*	SB	*CB*	*NB*	SB	*CB*	*NB*	SB	*CB*	*NB*
1840				*8*		51	*21*		69	*8*	16	53
1850	*10*	1	74	*11*		52	*20*	1	75	*11*	16	36
1860	*19*	9	41	*7*		50	*27*	12	48	*12*	24	17
1870	*27*	13	29	*7*	21	20	*33*	16	35	*14*	29	10
1880	*26*	16	17	*11*	26	15	*36*	18	29	*14*	35	8
1890	*25*	15	13	*15*	37	16	*34*	20	25	*19*	37	7
1900	*23*	18	11	*12*	50	9	*29*	30	20	*18*	50	6
1910	*19*	21	7	*16*	61	12	*30*	30	19	*19*	54	5

Source Hansen (1978), Pihkala (1978), Egge (1983) and Nygren (1985)

The Danish savings banks are a special case. Initially more than 90 per cent of their investments were placed in the government treasury. But from the late 1830s criticism against this system, not allowing the savings banks to meet the credit demands on the local credit markets, increased rapidly. In 1848 the Danish savings banks lost the right to place the saver's deposits in the treasury, and they almost immediately developed into major players on the local credit markets. Especially the rural savings banks made important contributions in the late nineteenth century to meet the demands of the swiftly developing agricultural sector of the Danish economy.[21]

Finally, the development of the Finnish savings banks had, as the whole Finnish economy, a rather slow and late starts in comparison to the other Nordic countries. The lack of demand, reflecting the general development level of the Finnish economy, during most of the nineteenth century clearly held back the development of the savings banks. On the other hand, the Finnish savings bank continued to gain markets shares during the twentieth century in a pace that surpasses their Nordic counterparts.[22]

In a somewhat wider, European perspective the investments and lending operations of the nineteenth century and early twentieth-century

[21] Hansen (1978) and (1982) and Clemmensen (1985).

[22] Pihkala (1978) and Kuusterä (1996).

savings banks seem to fall into two, rather separate categories. The savings banks in for example Great Britain, France and Belgium have been characterized as specialized in collecting the savings of the less-wealthy public, and foremost meant the growing working class. Considering the potentially rather wide range of financial services that banks could choose to offer its clients at this time, these categories of savings banks were merely passive deposit organizations, with hardly no active investment policies at all. Considering the savings banks' contribution to general economic development, to industrial growth and to urbanization, in these countries their role must be understood as one characterized first and foremost by passivity and inflexibility, albeit they did make important, but, however, indirect, contributions in collecting savings and redistributing them to other sectors of the economy.

There are some resemblances between the Nordic savings banks and the savings banks in Germany, Austria and Hungary, savings banks that constitute the other category of savings banks. These savings banks showed, in various degrees, several similarities with the commercial banks in regarding the character of the actual, daily businesses. It is possible to characterize the Nordic savings banks, with some partial exceptions regarding the Finnish savings banks, as even more banking- and credit-oriented, thus taking on the much more effort-demanding and risky task of financing different sectors of the local economies.

In analyzing *why and how* many of the savings banks in the Nordic countries developed into dynamic, risk-managing financial institutions on the local and regional credit markets, it is essential to include the structure of the general political system, and especially the relationship between local and regional public authorities and the governmental authorities on the national level. An inherent component in and characteristic of the political systems in all the Nordic countries, was a high level of local and regional independence. The national government had no ambitions, and no economic means, of interfering in detail in the development of a modernized banking and financial system. This encouraged, and essentially demanded, local and regional actors—including founding fathers and managers of savings banks—to acquire and to continuously develop skills in risk management. There was no alternative, if your savings bank was to survive. The national government was for sure not going to engage in any lender of last resort scheme, especially not in a financial organization that was not supposed to engage in any risky business.

References

Américi, L. (2002), "Preparing the People for Capitalism: Relations with Depositors in a French Savings Bank During the 1820s". *Financial History Review*, Vol. 9, pp. 5–19.

Bergström, K. (1916), "Belåning av bostadsfastigheter i Sverige år 1912". *Bostadskommisionens utredningar IV*. Stockholm.

Born, K.-E (1983), *International Banking in the 19th and 20th Centuries*. Warwickshire: Berg Publishers.

Brandal, T., Nerheim, G., & Nordvik H. (1989), *Penger spart – penger tjent: sparebanker og okonomisk utvikling på Sör-Vestlandet fra 1839–1989*. Stavanger: SR-bank.

Cameron, R. (1967), *Banking in the Early Stages of Development: A Study in Comparative Economic History*. New York: Oxford University Press.

Clemmensen, N. (1985), *Sparekassebevegelsen i Danmark 1810–1914*. Köbenhavn: Jurist- og ökonomförbundets förlag.

Collins, M. (1991). *Banks and Industrial Finance in Britain 1800–1939*. Basingstoke: Palgrave Macmillan.

Edwards, J., & Ogilvie, S. (1996). Universal Banks and German Industrialization: A Reappraisal. *Economic History Review, XLIX*, 427–446.

Egge, Å. (1983), "Transformation of Bank Structures in the Industrial Period: The Case of Norway 1830–1914". *Journal of European Economic History*, Vol. 12, pp. 271–294.

Fälting, L. (2001), *Småhusfinansiering. En studie av kommunens, statens och enskilda aktörers riskhantering i Nyköping 1904–1948*. Uppsala: Acta Universitatis Upsaliensis.

Hansen, S-Å. (1978), "Kreditformer og industriel vaekst i Danmark". In G Authén-Blom (Ed.), *Utviklingen av kredit tog kredittinstitusjoner i de nordiska land ca. 1850–1914*. Tapir: University of Trondheim.

Hansen, S.-Å. (1982), "The Transformation of Bank Structures in the Industrial Period: The Case of Denmark". *Journal of European Economic History*, Vol. 11, pp. 575–603.

Hellgren, H. (2003), *Fasta förbindelser. En studie av låntagare hos sparbanken och informella kreditgivare i Sala 1860–1910*. Uppsala: Acta Universitatis Upsaliensis.

Hollis, A., & Sweetman, A. (1998), "Microcredit in Prefamine Ireland". *Explorations in Economic History*, Vol. 35, pp. 347–380.

Horne, O. (1947), *A History of Savings Banks*. London/New York/Toronto: Oxford University Press.

Kuusterä, A. (1996), *Idé och pengar. Sparbankerna i det finländska samhället 1822–1994*. Helsingfors: Otava.

Lamoreaux, N. (1986), "Banks, Kinship and Economic Development: The New England Case". *Journal of Economic History*, Vol. XLVI, Issue 3, pp. 647–667.

Lamoreaux, N. (1991), "Information Problems and Banks' Specialization in Short-Term Commercial Lending: New England in the Nineteenth Century". In P. Temin (Ed.), *Inside the Business Enterprise: Historical Perspectives on the Use of Information*. Chicago and London: The University of Chicago Press.

Lamoreaux, N. (1994), *Insider Lending: Banks, Personal Connections and Economic Development in Industrial New England*. Cambridge: Cambridge University Press.

Lilja, K. (2004), *Marknad och hushåll. Sparande och krediter i Falun 1820–1910 utifrån ett livscykelperspektiv*. Uppsala: Acta Universitatis Upsaliensis.

Lindgren, H (2002), "The Modernization of Swedish Credit Markets, 1840–1905: Evidence from Probate Records". *The Journal of Economic History*, Vol. 62, Issue 3, pp. 810–832.

Nygren, I. (1967), *Svensk sparbanksutlåning 1820–1913*. Göteborg: Meddelanden från ekonomisk-historiska institutionen, Göteborgs universitet.

Nygren, I. (1970a), *Västsvenska sparbankers medelsplacering 1820–1913*. Göteborg: Meddelanden från ekonomisk-historiska institutionen, Göteborgs universitet.

Nygren, I. (1970b), *Svenska sparbankers medelsplacering 1914–1968*. Göteborg: Meddelanden från ekonomisk-historiska institutionen, Göteborgs universitet.

Nygren, I. (1981), *Svensk kreditmarknad 1820–1875. Översikt av det institutionella kreditväsendets utveckling*. Göteborg: Meddelanden från ekonomisk-historiska institutionen, Göteborgs universitet.

Nygren, I. (1983), "Transformation of Bank Structures in the Industrial Period: The Case of Sweden 1820–1913". *Journal of European Economic History*, Vol. 12, pp. 29–68.

Nygren, I. (1985), *Från Stockholms Banco till Citibank. Svensk kreditmarknad under 325 år*. Malmö: Liber förlag.

Nygren, I. (1987), *Göteborgs kreditmarknad 1820–1913*. Göteborg: Department of Economic History, Gothenburg University.

Ó Gráda, C. (2003), "Savings Banks as an Institutional Import: The Case of Nineteenth-Century Ireland". *Financial History Review*, Vol. 10, Issue 1, pp. 31–55.

Perlinge, A. (2005), *Sockenbankirerna. Kreditrelationer och tidig bankverksamhet. Vånga socken i Skåne 1840–1900*. Stockholm: Nordiska museets förlag.

Petersson, T. (2000), "Playing It Safe? Lending Policies of the Savings Bank in Nyköping, 1832–1875". In L Fälting et al., *Both a Borrower and a Lender Be: Savings Banks in the Economic Development of Sweden 1820–1939*. Uppsala: Uppsala Papers in Financial History, Uppsala University.

Petersson, T. (2001), *Framväxten av ett lokalt banksystem. Oppunda sparbank, Södermanlands enskilda bank och stationssamhället Katrineholm 1850–1916*. Uppsala: Acta Universitatis Upsaliensis.

Pihkala, E. (1978), "Kredit och kreditformer i Finland, 1840–1914". In G Authén-Blom (Ed.), *Utviklingen av kredit tog kredittinstitusjoner i de nordiska land ca. 1850–1914*. Tapir: University of Trondheim.

Ross, D. (2002), "'Penny Banks' in Glasgow, 1850–1914". *Financial History Review*, Vol. 9, pp. 21–39.

Sjölander, A. (2003), *Den naturliga ordningen. Makt och intressen i de svenska sparbankerna 1882–1968*. Uppsala: Acta Universitatis Upsaliensis.

Skånland, H. (1967), *The Norwegian Credit Market Since 1900*. Oslo: Aschehoug.

Thomes, P. (1995), "German Savings Banks as Instruments of Regional Development Up to the Second World War". In Y. Cassis, G. Feldman, & U. Olsson (Eds.), *The Evolution of Financial Institutions and Markets in Twentieth Century Europe*. London.

Thue, L. (2014), *Forandring og forankring. Sparebankene i Norge 1822–2014*. Oslo: Universitetsforlaget.

Tomka, B. (2002), "The Development of Hungarian Banking, 1880–1931: An International Comparison". *Journal of European Economic History*, Vol. 31, pp. 125–162.

CHAPTER 6

Trust and Mistrust: Practical Aspects of Risk Management and Lending

Abstract The local savings bank's market in the town of Gävle is presented. The organization of the local credit system is discussed as well as the composition of the board of directors in Gävle savings bank. The consequences of savings banks legislation and the principle of credit granting are analyzed, as well as the structural difference between accepted and rejected loan applications. The development of credits, insider lending, collaterals, interest rates and risk management is discussed.

Keyword Local credit market · Legislation · Credit structure · Credit risks · Interest rates · Local networks · Rejected applications

This chapter deals with the development of lending in Gävle Savings bank (*Gevle Stads Sparbank*) in the late nineteenth century. The aim is not to present a long-term development analysis, but a micro study of the principles behind lending in a local community. The market for Gävle Savings Bank was foremost concentrated to the town of Gävle, while the surrounding county mostly was handled by the Gävle County Savings bank (*Gevleborgs Läns Sparbank*). However, the Gävle Savings

M. Larsson et al., *Risk Management in Early Banking*, Palgrave Studies in the History of Finance,
https://doi.org/10.1007/978-3-030-80775-7_6

Bank was not the only financial institute in Gävle. The commercial *Gefleborgs Enskilda Bank* had been established in 1864 and held a strong position in the market for business credits. The period for analysis is the first half of the 1890s (1990, 1991, 1993 and 1994), and there is a good reason for that. In 1892 a new savings banks legislation was introduced, which meant increased guidance of the savings banks' economic administration.

The basis for this analysis is the bookkeeping of the Gävle Savings Bank, and especially the books for credits, where all loan applications were registered. These books included not only information about the loan applicant, but also the discussion held by the savings banks credit committee/executive board. Usually, in other savings banks this detailed information has either been destroyed or disappeared for other reason. This makes it possible to get a unique insight in the bank's credit management and in how the banks executive board reasoned about risks when granting credits.

Gävle—A Town in Transition

The origin of Gävle goes back to the fourteenth century when a village was established at the mouth of the Gavle stream into the Baltic see. The favourable geographical position made it possible for Gävle to develop as a major harbour for trade with iron-products as well as timber and wood. But royal restrictions introduced already in the 1350s hampered trade from harbours north of Stockholm. However, compared to other towns and villages along the Baltic coast, Gävle had a privileged position, for example as an export harbour. The neighbouring countryside was also requested to carry out all trade and other commercial activities in Gävle and not on any local market. In exchange for this the Gävle merchants payed a regular tax to the crown.

The town obviously had a privileged position compared to several other towns in the northern part of Sweden, and it sometimes even competed with Stockholm as the centre for Swedish trade in the Baltic see. However, after complains from the Stockholm merchants, the already strict policy controlling trade from the northern part of Sweden was sharpened, and in the seventeenth and early eighteenth century this affected Gävle's position, as direct export from Gävle was prohibited.[1]

The economic situation for Gävle improved in the latter half of eighteenth century and after the war with Russia in the early nineteenth century, both trade and production developed. From the 1850s several industries were established connection with the towns old traditions in wood- and iron-industries, but also in more private consumption-oriented production (see also Chapter 2). In the southern part of the town different iron and other metal industries developed, producing agriculture machinery, ships and tools as well as heaters and cookers.[2]

The northern part of Gävle was dominated by new companies in textile and leather industries. Of special importance was *Gefle Manufactur* established in 1849, by among others the local entrepreneur Per Murén, who also was engaged in the establishment of the local railway (*Gävle-Dala Järnväg*) connecting the countryside in the west of Gävle with the town in 1859. *Gävle Manufactur* factory was constructed with British plants as blueprints, concentrating on cotton spinning and weaving. Other textile industries were founded in 1862 (*Gefle Ångväveri*) and in 1874 (*Gefle ullspinneri och trikåfabrik*), the later manufacturing wool products.[3]

During the 1850s, 1860s and 1870s glass and ceramic production were started in Gävle, and in 1899 a new sawmill was established near the *Gävle* harbour. Several companies were later started in this area as the harbour also moved away from the town centre and closer to Baltic see. The harbour became increasingly important for the wooden industry as well as other companies producing for markets outside the local region.

The "industrialization" of Gävle was slowed down in connection with the large fire in 1869, but this also opened for investments in the building of new dwellings and business premises, which stimulated the local economy. After the fire, a new city plan was introduced which included boulevards through the town and regulations on buildings especially in the centre of the town. This meant the building of large stone houses instead of small wooden houses. However, a pre-condition for

[1] Arbell (1946) and Hellner (1946).

[2] Elfstrand (1946a), Arbell and Humbla (1948), Gårdlund et al. (1973) and www.gavlevarv.se.

[3] Karlström (1974) and www.gavledraget.com.

Table 6.1 The population in Gävle 1870–1910

Year	*Population*
1870	13,822
1880	18,758
1890	23,484
1900	29,522
1910	35,202
1920	37,761

Source *Historical statistics of Sweden Part 1. Population*

this development was heavy investment in both infrastructure and houses, which continued well into the 1890s.

The fast development of Gävle towards the late nineteenth century, can also be seen in the growth of population (Table 6.1). Between 1870 and 1900 the population more than doubled and especially during the 1890s the expansion was extensive. Population growth continued also during the first decades of the twentieth century. Even though the town's population seems low in an international comparison, Gävle was the fifth largest town in Sweden by the turn of the century 1900.

The economy of Gävle was dominated by local societies—organizations created by different occupational groups. Originally there were five societies, of which four were connected to specific occupations—the commerce society, the craftsmen's society, the fishermen's society, and the ship masters and owners' society. The fifth society was made up of the local upper class—persons having important positions in the town such as teachers, physicians, and military employees. From the eighteenth century these societies took an active part in the administration of the town, but this changed after a new municipal law was introduced in 1862. With this democratization reform the role of the societies was broken. However, they still played a role in coordinating the interest of special groups and develop new production activities in the town. The societies also appointed representatives to the board of the local savings bank until 1893.[4]

[4] Arbell (1946, pp. 316–317).

Table 6.2 Society groups represented at the Gävle Savings Bank executive board up to 1893 and after

	1888–1893	*1894*
Upper class' society	3	
Commerce society	3	
Craftsmen society	2	
Fishermens' society	1	
Factory owner's society	1	
Principals	2	12

Source Fyhrvall (1904)

Gävle Savings Bank

Gävle savings bank was founded in 1824 as the 24th savings bank in Sweden. Like other savings banks established in the first formation wave, Gävle savings bank had its primary customers among people in or close to the town. This meant that lending probably from the beginning came in favour of craftsmen, small industries, and other local investors.

The Gävle savings bank was established through an initiative from the owner of a local merchant house with the help of the governor of Gävle county. From the start, the commerce society and the upper class' society played a major role in the development of the savings bank. The banks principals were of course important for the establishment, but the executive board was elected by the five societies, which were appointed by the principals, where the upper class' society and the commerce society had the largest representation (Table 6.2).[5] This organizational structure was kept until 1894, when it was replaced by a direct election from the principals.[6] The implications of this were marginal. Initially, more or less the same persons as before were on the savings banks board. That is not surprising, since the principals as the creators had a central role to play in all the savings banks activities.

Towards the end of the nineteenth century, the local societies had lost most of their importance and were reorganized as more traditional interest groups. But the reorganization of the savings banks executive

[5] The society of ship masters and owners participated in the establishment of the savings bank in 1824. However, it was reorganized in the 1870s and discontinued in the 1880s. The factory owner's society was represented on the saving bank's executive board from the late 1860s.

[6] Fyhrvall (1904).

board was also a consequence of the new savings banks law in 1892 (in force from 1893), which stated that the banks principals should represent the depositors and supervise both the administration and the board. According to the charter the banks board should consist of 12 ordinary members and three deputy members. However, the most important consequence of this new regulation was that the savings bank no longer had to declare their activities to the town's magistrate.[7]

From the start local dignitaries played a major role in Gävle savings bank's business. With representatives from the largest industrial companies and shipowners in Gävle as well as the Governor, the aim was to establish the necessary trust to obtain the savers' interest in depositing in the savings bank. The organizational structure with representatives from all local societies on the bank's executive board probably helped to retain the general confidence in the savings bank. Several of the board representatives in the 1890s also held other important positions in the political and economic life of Gävle, for example, the chief district judge and the towns chief architect, who was important in the planning of Gävle's expansion and the construction of new houses. Credits for the building of new houses and dwellings were also the most important area for the savings bank's lending. The executive board members were all men.[8]

The financial market in Gävle was also developed through the establishment of commercial banks, where especially *Gefleborgs Enskilda Bank* played an important role for the financing of the fast growing commercial and industrial activities. In 1863 a new savings bank was also organized for the rural areas of Gävle county.[9] Thus, there was a boundary between the two savings banks markets, but this did not mean that Gävle savings bank was prevented from accepting deposits or granting credits to persons or companies from applicants outside Gävle. On the contrary, around 1/3 of the Gävle savings bank's credits during the first half of the 1890s was granted to borrowers outside Gävle.[10]

The last two decades of the nineteenth century meant a fast growth of both population and the size of Gävle's urban area. A well-functioning financial market was the basis for this development, which of course also

[7] Fyhrvall (1904).

[8] Fyhrvall (1904).

[9] Fyhrvall (1913).

[10] Gävle stads sparbank, Styrelsens lånehandlingar 1890–1891 and 1893–1894.

involved Gävle savings bank. Deposits increased especially fast during the last years of the 1880s and between 1894 and 1899. Between 1885 and 1899 deposits more than doubled, from 2.7 to 5.5 million SEK. This growth was a prerequisite for the expansion of the savings bank's lending. But lending also increased because of a new policy adopted by the savings bank's executive board, which meant that a larger part of the deposits was used for credits. In 1885, 63 per cent of deposits were used for lending, while the share had increased to 80 per cent in 1899 (Fig. 6.1, see also Chapter 4).

The new approach towards the bank's risk management is also demonstrated by the administration of the bank's assets. Deposits in other banks had since the early 1880s played an important role for the bank's capital management. However, in the early 1890s deposits in other banks dropped sharply, while credits increased in importance (Fig. 6.2). Most likely, this reflects the growth of Gävle and the increased demand for credits. This also corresponds with the general development of the Swedish savings bank (see Chapter 5).

From an overall perspective, Gävle savings bank appears to have taken larger risks in the 1890s compared to the previous decade. However, risks can not only be evaluated from aggregate data. We must look behind this

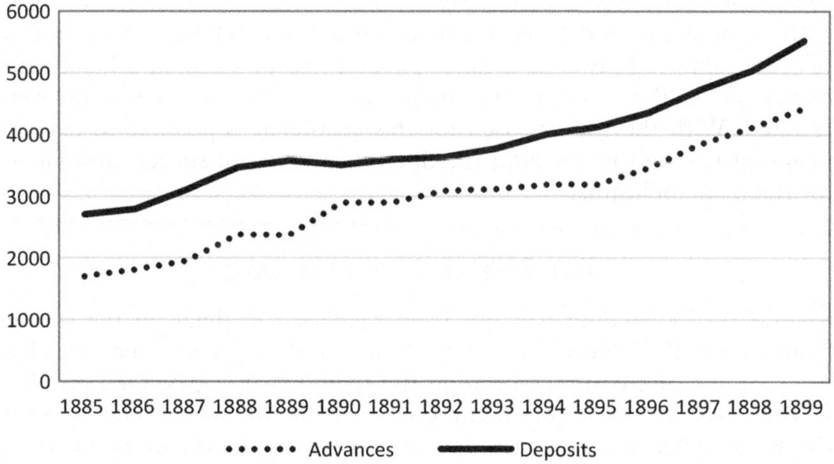

Fig. 6.1 Deposits and advances in Gävle savings bank 1885–1899 in thousand SEK (*Sources* SOS, sparbanksstatistik 1895–1901; Nygren 1967)

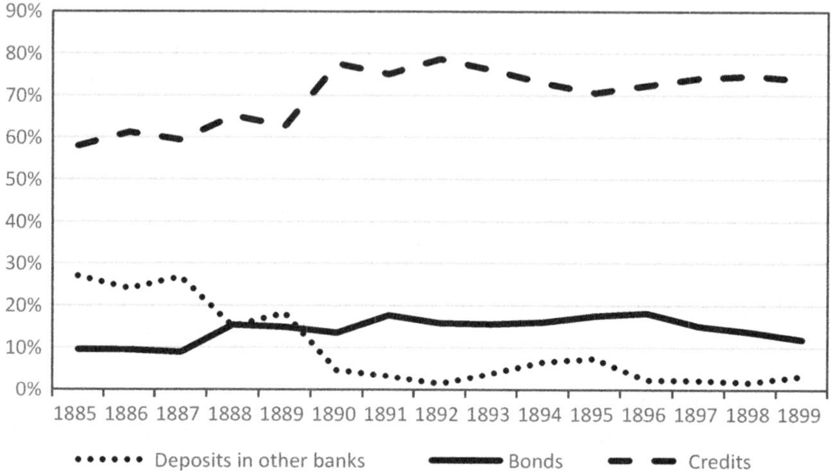

Fig. 6.2 Gävle Savings bank's management of assets as per cent of total assets (*Sources* SOS, sparbanksstatistik 1895–1901; Nygren 1967)

information and assess each individual credit engagement and follow up the use of collaterals as well as interest rates to compensate for increased risks. The new savings banks' law in 1892 might also have influenced Gävle savings bank's risk management. Thus, the handling and acceptance of credit applications is of great importance to understand a bank's risk management. But of even larger importance is why some applicants were rejected. With the sources used for this chapter it is possible to have an image of this and understand the difference between success and failure for the loan applicants.

The Use of Collaterals

Savings banks' lending had not been regulated in detail in the savings bank law of 1875. However, the discussion about regulative measures had been intense and continued during the following decades. One problem was the existence of insider lending to board members and employees in the bank. This discussion resulted in a new regulation in 1890 which prohibited lending to members of the banks' executive board and to banks' officials, except for loans against adequate securities (shares and bonds) as collateral. The same persons were also prohibited from guaranteeing other persons lending.[11] These restrictions were aiming to reduce the internal lending which had developed in some savings banks (see Chapter 5). But this did not stop employees and board members from applying and accepting credits in other savings banks. This explains why bank employees can be found among the borrowers in Gävle savings bank.

In May 1891, a Royal committee was appointed to overhaul savings banks' legislation and one of the important questions was what kind of collaterals that should be accepted. Above all the use of name collaterals was criticized for being too risky. However, the committee saw this as a problem for the largest savings bank, while the smaller banks had this under control. Most of the lending in these were granted with name as collateral and since the banks had good control over applicants within their geographical market, this was no problem. If the use of names as collateral was prohibited, a person's good name might be replaced by a bad mortgage collateral, which would make lending riskier.[12] Therefore this restriction was not accepted in the savings banks' legislation of 1892. However, it was obvious that lending against name as collateral was not especially popular in the committee and that an inadequate control of the guarantors could result in higher lending risks.

Lending against mortgage collaterals was also under discussion, but no restriction against this lending was regarded, as necessary. However, one regulative measure indirectly had implications for the savings banks. Mortgages on real estate could—up to 50 per cent of the assessed value—be accepted as a part of the banks' reserve funds. Thus, these credits could be included in the compulsory accumulation of reserve capital and release other assets for lending or other investments.[13] As a consequence, interest rates could be reduced for credits up to 50 per cent of the assessed value, while higher mortgages needed larger interest rates.

In Gävle savings bank, as in other savings banks, the executive board was liable for all the banks' credits. However, in Gävle, smaller credits with good collaterals, could be handled by the managing director and in hindsight be accepted by the executive board. The board had their meetings each Friday—except on national holidays—to ventilate loan applications

[11] *SFS 1892:59*, Lag angående sparbanker.

[12] Sommarin (1942, pp. 315–318).

[13] SFS 1892:59, Lag angående sparbanker.

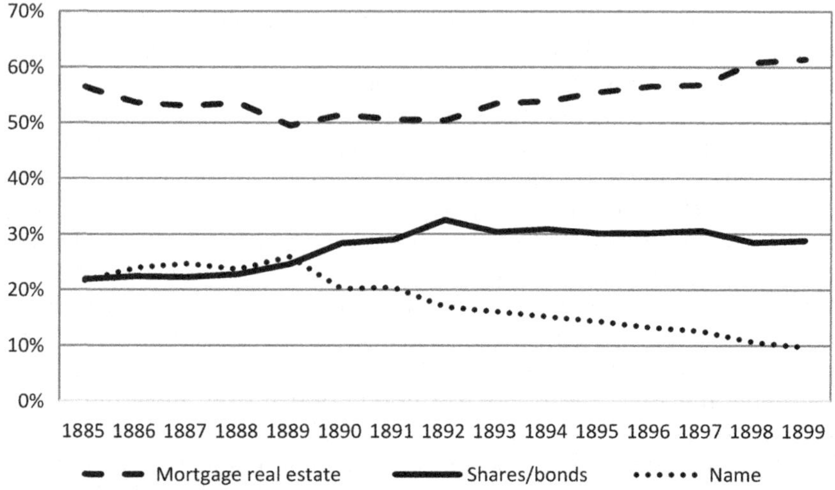

Fig. 6.3 Gävle savings bank's total lending allocated on different collaterals 1885–1899 (*Sources* SOS, sparbanksstatistik 1895–1901; Nygren 1967)

and other board affairs. Among important preparations before these meetings, were the evaluation of the risks connected with the applicant as well as the value of mortgages and the creditworthiness of guarantors. This information was prepared by the managing director as well as members of the executive board, but also by "trustworthy" persons outside Gävle when the applicant was resident outside the town.[14]

Even though the legislation of 1892 did not include any comprehensive changes of the lending regulation, the new law and especially the discussion of the role of saving banks in Sweden's economy had a serious impact.[15] This can be seen in Gävle savings bank during the 1890s, when name collaterals as part of total lending fell from 26 per cent in 1889 to 10 per cent in 1899. At the same time, the use of shares and bonds as collaterals as well as mortgages increased (Fig. 6.3).

[14] Gävle stads sparbank, F 1a lånehandlingar 1890–1891 and 1893–1894.

[15] After the legislation of 1892 it became more obvious that lending to the growing industry and trade was to be handled by commercial banks, while savings banks had a role in promoting the savings of ordinary people and handle less risky credits and capital investments in for example bonds. See Larsson (2010) and Sjölander (2003).

This increased role of mortgage collaterals in total lending can partially be explained by a larger number of mortgage loans, but also on the increased size of these loans compared to loans with name collateral. The expansion of Gävle as an industrial and trading town assumed these larger credits.

An analysis shows that the annual loan applications exhibit a stability especially for applications with name collaterals—even though December month is missing from the 1894 sources. Mortgage loans on the other hand dropped considerably in 1894 (Table 6.3). This could be a consequence of the high number of applications in 1891, when applications with mixed collaterals peaked. There are good reasons to believe that name collaterals would be stable between the years. Most of these applications were small and not directly coordinated with changes in the local economy, while applications with mortgage were large and linked to the development of Gävle.

The number of loan rejections was relatively stable between the years, both absolutely and relatively (Table 6.4). Rejections between 15 and 18 per cent of the applications can hardly be regarded as exceptional. However, of larger interest is the distribution of rejections between different collaterals. The lowest rejection rate was for shares and bonds, which is not unexpected since the provisions were clear and easily adjustable to all applications. The rejections of applications with mortgage collaterals were also low, except for 1890 (Table 6.5), when credits with mixed collaterals were exceptionally low. But it is difficult to detect any structural reasons for this, instead it requires a closer analysis of each rejection.

The largest number of loan rejections were connected to name collaterals. Since the interpretation of the credit roles for this type of loans had the highest feasibility, it is hardly surprising that rejections overall were the largest. Rejections were an effective way for the executive board to avoid asymmetric information. But it is important to examine this result more closely. This will be done later in this chapter.

The height of interest rates reflects the regulations from 1892, where rates for name collaterals were supposed to be higher than both shares and mortgages. However, interest rates for loans with name collateral were already higher in 1890 and 1891. Shares and bonds on the other hand were regarded as the least risky collateral with an interest of 4.5 per cent (Table 6.6). These credits could be given up to the nominal value of these

Table 6.3 Number of loan applications in Gävle savings bank 1890–1891 and 1893–1894

	Mortage		*Name*		*Mortage/name*		*Shares/bonds*		*Total*
	Approvals	*Rejections*	*Approvals*	*Rejections*	*Approvals*	*Rejections*	*Approvals*	*Rejections*	*Approvals*
1890	104	25	87	20	20	3	10	0	269
1891	116	13	82	27	39	7	29	1	314
1893	107	11	78	25	21	10	17	1	270
1894	61	10	82	2 4	22	9	23	0	231

Sources Gävle stads sparbank, F1a lånehandlingar (loan books) 1890–1891 and 1893–1894
Note Loan applications for December 1894 are missing

Table 6.4 Loan rejections, absolute and relative numbers 1890–1891 and 1893–1893–1894

	Number av rejections	*Rejections/total applications in %*
1890	48	17.8
1891	48	15.3
1893	47	17.4
1894	43	18.6

Sources Gävle stads sparbank, F1a lånehandlingar (loan books) 1890–1891 and 1893–1894

Table 6.5 Approved and rejected loan applications allocated in per cent on different types of collaterals 1890–1891 and 1893–1894

	Mortage		*Name*		*Mortage/name*		*Shares/bonds*	
	Approvals	*Rejections*	*Approvals*	*Rejections*	*Approvals*	*Rejections*	*Approvals*	*Rejections*
1890	28.7	9.3	32.4	7.4	7.4	1.1	3.7	0
1891	27.0	4.1	26.2	8.6	12.4	2.2	9.2	0.3
1893	39.6	4.1	28.9	9.3	7.8	3.7	6.3	0.3
1894	26.4	4.3	35.5	10.4	9.5	3.9	10.0	0

Sources Gävle stads sparbank, F1a lånehandlingar (loan books) 1890–1891 and 1893–1894

Table 6.6 Interest rates for different collaterals in per cent 1890–1891 and 1893–1894

	Interest rate in per cent
Shares/Bonds	4.5
Property mortgage	4.5–5.0
Mixed collaterals (name/property mortgage)	5.5
Name	5.5

Sources Gävle stads sparbank, F1a lånehandlingar (loan books) 1890–1891 and 1893–1894

securities. But this was not necessarily taken for granted. Shares in well-known Swedish companies registered on the Stockholm stock exchange often had a higher market price than the nominal value. But on the other hand, it was much harder to obtain a reliable market price for shares in local companies. However, the bank preferred to have the same rules for all shares. The shares most commonly used as collaterals in Gävle were in banks and railway companies, often with a local connection.

Property mortgages had an interest rate of 4.5 or 5 per cent. The lowest rate was most frequently used in 1890 and 1894 and preferably for owners of large industries with established companies and comparatively high credits. But in 1894 farms which did not have any mortgage loans were also given these low interest rates. A special credit engagement with the lowest interest rate of 4 per cent, was given to Gävle Kindergarten in 1894. This low rate might well be a consequence of the savings banks social mission—which had been lifted in the 1892 legislation.

Interest rates of 5 per cent for property mortgages were only given for up to 50 per cent of the fire insurance value, which was used instead of the assessed value. Credits over 50 per cent of the fire insurance value had to be complemented with additional collaterals. Beside mortgage, these mixed collaterals consisted of guarantees from at least two "trustworthy" persons. The interest rate would then be increased to 5.5 per cent. But if the credits were divided in two parts, with one covering up to 50 per cent of the fire insurance value, the interest rate for this part could be set at 5 per cent. Name collaterals always had an interest rates of 5.5 per cent. For the loan applicant the most important was to find good names to guarantee the application, otherwise it would be rejected.

It is obvious that Gävle savings bank had elaborated distinct rules for their credit system, which from an overall perspective evaluated the risks connected with the size of credits and the collaterals. Even though the legislation of 1892 had not specified any regulations for banks' lending, the handling of credits in Gävle savings bank is consistent with the discussion preceded the legislation. The prohibition for savings banks to grant credits to executive board members and employees was upheld by the bank. There were also no cases when board members acted as guarantors for credit applications.

Trust and Mistrust—The Structure of Borrowers and Loan Rejections

The structure of Gävle savings bank's lending was closely related to the structure of industry and commerce, but also to Gävle's position as an important administrative town. Another aspect of Gävle's economy was the limited importance of agriculture. Most of the farms surrounding the town had a limited size and their production was allocated on a local market. Thus, the need for investments in agriculture was limited, which

Table 6.7 Borrowers distributed in per cent on different categories

	1890	*1891*	*1893*	*1894*
Agriculture	2.1	3.0	6.8	4.8
Shopkeepers and whole-sale dealers	9.1	7.8	6.0	5.3
Craftsmen and artisans	17.7	21.4	18.1	15.9
Public servants and local authorities	18.2	10.4	7.2	12.6
Shipping and transport	12.8	12.2	11.7	12.6
Blue-collar workers	9.6	14.3	21.9	18.8
White-collar workers	11.2	11.7	14.3	12.6
Companies	1.6	3.0	1.9	1.0
Others	17.7	16.2	12.1	16.4

Sources Gävle stads sparbank, F1a lånehandlingar (loan books) 1890–1891 and 1893–1894

is shown by the relatively low importance of borrowers from the agriculture sector (Table 6.7). This is also clear in comparison with the town of Nyköping, where not only small farmers were borrowers, but also large landowners (see Chapter 5).

As a centre for the surrounding region, and as an administrative town for the northern part of Sweden, Gävle had traditionally been an important town for trade and commerce. But as the industry grew the relative role of shopkeepers and whole-sale dealers fell—including as borrowers in the savings bank. Craftsmen and artisans had a stable position among the savings bank's borrowers, with close to 20 per cent of the granted loans in the early 1890s. However, a clear sign of the growing industrialization in Gävle was the increased importance of borrowers from blue-collar workers (Table 6.7). Among both craftsmen and blue-collar workers, we find people involved in the building industry, such as building constructors, carpenters, bricklayers and building workers. These workers constituted a large part of the savings bank's borrowers in the early 1890s. It is difficult to be precise about the role of building activities for the Gävle savings bank lending. Mortgage loans as well as mixed collateral loans were related to housing and building activities, but several loans with name collaterals were also connected to the building industry. This is proved by the preparation of loan applications to the bank's executive board meetings.

Among the important borrowers were also white-collar workers and people employed by the state or local authorities. The first group consisted mostly of industrialist and people employed at the business' offices. In the second group employees from the local municipality and the church played a distinctive role. Several officers from the local regiments were also among the borrowers.

The group of uncategorized borrowers were stable and one of the largest customers groups. This group was dominated by widows, of which some had taken over their husbands' companies, while others probably had other occupations or held properties that were supportive. Since these widows often were in possession of a house or a farm, they could relatively easily obtain credits from the bank. The female borrowers accounted for around ten per cent the savings bank's credit applications.

It is obvious that the companies in Gävle foremost used other bank contacts than Gävle savings bank. There were only 2–7 loan application from companies per year during the period of investigation. A few of these companies were reoccurring during several years. But even though they were few, their credits were often large, and therefore they were important customers.

An overview of Gävle savings bank's credits implies that lending reached a large part of the society. Credits were not only for the well-off but included ordinary workers, small farmers, and retired people. The primary issue was if the loan applicant could provide either a good mortgage or name collateral.

Craftsmen, artisans, and blue-collar workers were important for Gävle savings bank's lending—compared to several other saving banks. However, a crucial question is if the rejections were higher for working class applicants than for well-off applicants. An analysis of the relative rejection rate shows that applications from the agricultural sector—with 2.1—were over-represented, as was shopkeepers and whole-sale dealers as well as companies (Table 6.8).[16] In contrast, public servants, local authorities and especially blue-collar workers had a lower representation among rejected applications.

This indicates that applicants from the working class were not discouraged because of their social position. Another explanation for the low representation of rejected applicants from both blue-collar workers and

[16] Relative rejection rate = relative importance of rejected applications per categories in per cent/relative importance of categories in per cent. Values of 1 means that the number of rejections equals the categories importance among total borrowers. Values under 1 means that the categories are undervalued, while values over 1 means that the categories are overvalued among rejections.

Table 6.8 Relative rejection rate 1890–1891 and 1893–1894

Agriculture	2.1
Shopkeepers and whole-sale dealers	1.6
Craftsmen and artisans	1.1
Public servants and local authorities	0.8
Shipping and transport	1.1
Blue-collar workers	0.7
White-collar workers	0.9
Companies	1.3
Others	0.7

Source Calculations based on Gävle stads sparbank, F1a lånehandlingar (loan books) 1890–1891 and 1893–1894

the group of others, is that their applications consisted of small loans while applications from white-collar workers, companies as well as some agricultural loan applications were considerably higher.

The preparations of loan applications preceding the executive board meetings were both detailed and important. The applicants had an initial meeting with representatives from the bank and formulated a complete application. Necessary information about the mortgage as well as guarantors were collected after which representatives from the bank made evaluations of both the applicants and guarantors. To assist with this, the bank used both the executive board and a network of contact persons and organizations in and close to Gävle, such as the police, teachers, and clergymen.

The situation became more complicated when loan applications came from persons outside the immediate Gävle area. However, even in these cases, contacts were established with local authorities or persons. Both the applicants and the guarantors were controlled in the same way. The information was compiled in the executive board's loan book by the managing director and a recommendation of approval or rejection was formulated.[17]

These loan books give us the opportunity to compare rejected applications with accepted ones and hopefully establish what parameters could be a burden for an application. From the analysis of all loans for the period 1890–1891 and 1893–1894, it has been possible to identify problematic areas in the handling of new credits.

[17] Sources: Gävle stads sparbank, F1a lånehandlingar (loan books) 1890–1891 and 1893–1894.

One of the most important reasons why an application could not be accepted, was that it did not reach the requirements of the bank's formal regulations. For mortgage loans this meant that mortgages over 50 per cent of the fire insurance value had to be complemented with other collateral—bonds, shares or guarantors. In most cases, name collaterals were used. However, it was not unusual that applications without extra collaterals were too large and therefore rejected. This regulation was handled quite strictly. Of 59 rejected mortgage loans 1890–1891 and 1893–1894, 43 (73 per cent) were higher than 50 per cent of the value of the fire insurance, and thus rejected. In addition, 29 applications with mixed collaterals were rejected as a consequence of the combination of too high mortgage and insufficient name collaterals.[18]

While the use of mortgage collaterals had strict rules, the use of name collaterals was based on the evaluation of not only the applicant but also the guarantors. The evaluation of the applicant's possibility to fulfil payments was based on the personal knowledge of the executive board members and of those contacts that these persons had. This information was discussed at the board meeting and resulted in the board's decision. This discussion is sometimes referred to in the loan book, but more often there are no comments—which might indicate that the decision was not problematic. But when comments were included, they were often very straightforward, both when a loan was approved and when it was rejected. Positive comments could be formulated like "The applicant is a solid person, and his mother is well-off".[19] When a loan was rejected the information was also easy to grasp: "The applicant can only be granted 2,000 SEK, not 3,000",[20] or when information was a bit outside the scope of risk evaluation "His mother is a drunkard".[21]

Since both mortgage loans and loans with name collaterals were used for the building and reparation of houses, it was necessary to carry out an inspection of the object. The executive board not only visited the building sites but also made detailed estimations of planned rental income when the house was finished. It was clear that this information was important

[18] Sources: Gävle stads sparbank, F1a lånehandlingar (loan book) 1 890–1891 and 1893–1894.

[19] Loan book 1891, application 119.

[20] Loan book 1890, application 48.

[21] Loan book 1893, application 281.

for the decision, but it is difficult to see what requirements were needed for the loan to be approved. However, some comments were clear and resulted in loan approvals, such as "This is a first class building"[22] and "The town's architect approves this credit".[23]

The number of guarantors varied—between 2 and 10—with the size of the loan application. It is difficult to understand why some loans had several guarantors while others did not. This might have been the applicants' decision but could also have been the result of requests from the bank. The general practice was that loan applications less than 1000 SEK required two good guarantors. The sum of 1000 SEK may seem small, but it corresponds to 345,000 SEK in the value of 2020, or 2 year's salary for an industrial worker during the first half of 1890s. This made even small credits important, especially if there were lots of them. This explains why the bank was eager to evaluate all credit applications from the lowest of 100 SEK to the largest. The banks interest in guarantors can be seen in the following quotations: "This guarantor is no good"[24] or "One of the guarantors is good for 1,000 SEK, while the other is very fragile".[25]

The number of loan guarantors often increased with the size of the credit application. This was reasonable and probably encouraged by bank. There was no set size of how large a guarantee one single person could handle—of course that depended on the person—but an average of 500–800 SEK seems to be a normal sum. However, several guarantors were not a guarantee for a credit approval. An iron merchandiser applied for 1500 SEK with 8 guarantors in 1894, but his application was denied without comments in the loan book.[26] But when the regional police chief applied for 5000 SEK with 10 guarantors, the application was accepted.[27]

A guarantor's value was closely connected to the person's assets. Thus, a guarantor with a house or farm could more easily be accepted by the bank, which was especially important for larger credits. Often the evaluation of the guarantors was as comprehensive as that of the applicant,

[22] Loan book 1892, application 213.

[23] Loan book 1893, application 8.

[24] Loan book 1893, application 87.

[25] Loan book 1894, application 238.

[26] Loan book 1894, application 75.

[27] Loan book 1893, application 108.

as: "The guarantors are not property owners".[28] On the other hand, the evaluation sometimes could be done to hastily: "Proper men all of them, but the only asset they have are children".[29]

The choice of guarantors was not always made under the best circumstances. It could be difficult to find a person that was both wealthy enough and at the same time willing to be a guarantor. A large number of the applications therefore included guarantors from the same workplace as the applicant or from the same village. This was not ideal from the risk perspective and the bank seems to have avoided putting all the "eggs" in the same basket even for individual loans. There are also examples where several persons from the same village at the same time applied for credits with partly the same guarantors—all applications were then rejected.[30] This situation resembles what happened in another savings bank about 110 kms from Gävle, where hundreds of borrowers and guarantors were intricately connected with one another in a large network of credit relations. This was a fragile system and a couple of large individual failures could have threatened the entire local financial system (see Chapter 5).[31]

Another problem which endangered the traditional credit system in Gävle was the number of distant applications from—sometimes—faraway places from Gävle.[32] In some cases it has been possible to trace the applicants personal contacts to Gävle, though the person was resident elsewhere. But the problem was when the guarantors came from different parts of the country. The bank than used their contacts with mostly the church and the local police for information, but they could not always make contact and get the information they wanted. It has been possible to identify 21 rejected credit applications during the investigated period, which could have been linked to the geographical distance from Gävle and consequently the lack of reliable information. It is reasonable for a representative from Gävle savings bank to ask why the applicant did not

[28] Loan book 1893, application 75.

[29] Loan book 1891, application 317.

[30] Loan book 1891, applications 127, 131 and 133.

[31] Hellgren (2003).

[32] The so called "church tower principle" was common in savings banks and meant that the banks credit engagement should not reach longer than you still could see your customers from the church tower. This made it possible for the bank to know and monitor their borrowers.

use a local savings bank or if the application already had been rejected there.

The possibility of compensating higher risks in lending with increased interest rates was small. The rate levels had been set in advance for different types of loans and collaterals, and there is no example in the analyzed years of risk compensation through higher rates. This made the evaluation of applicants and collaterals increasingly important.

Conclusions

The Gävle savings bank was without doubt a legitimate actor on the local financial market in the early 1890s. After 65 years of active business and with an organization that was based on the representation of different groups in the local society, the savings bank ought to have received a general trust in the community. The expansion of deposits and advances in the 1880s and 1890s also confirm this. An extensive part of this expansion was also connected with the growth of the population and economy of Gävle.

The expansion of Gävle's industry and its development as a centre for transportation north and south as well as west in Sweden and to the international market gave the town its central position. The fast growth in the 1890s stimulated the building of a new town centre in Gävle as well as the construction of new dwellings. Consequently, deposits in Gävle savings bank grew from 3.5 million SEK in 1890 to over 4 million SEK in 1894.[33] The expansion was also apparent in the savings bank' s lending, which in the early 1890s was focussed on the reparation and construction of new buildings—both with mortgages and guarantors as collateral.

The risks connected with these credits were limited, since mortgage loans only were approved up to half of the fire insurance value, without additional collaterals. Together with a rigorous control of the applicants and their properties the risks connected with mortgage loans were quite low. The situation was different for credits against name collaterals. This type of credits still played an important role in Gävle savings bank's business in the middle of the 1890s–despite name collaterals being criticized for being too risky.

[33] Nygren (1967).

The social structure of Gävle savings banks lending was comparatively open towards borrowers from the working class and less privileged people. The use of mortgage loan was not uncommon among these groups, although the use of name collaterals dominated. The most important issue for these groups as well those well-off was to commit guarantors with properties that could be accepted by the bank´s executive board.

References

Online Sources

www.gavledraget.com.
www.gavlevarv.se.

Unpublished Sources

Arkiv Gävleborg (Gävle community archive) Gävle stads sparbank, F1a lånehandlingar 1890–1891 and 1893–1894 (Gävle savings bank, loan books).

Published Sources

SFS 1892:59, Lag angående sparbanker (Savings banks legislation).

Literature

Arbell, G. (1946), "Manufakturer och industrier". In N. S. Norling, G. E. Lundén, & P. Humbla, *Ur Gävle stads historia*. Gävle.
Arbell, G., & Humbla, P. (1948), *Båt- och fartygsbygge kring Gavleåns mynning*. Gävle: Gävle varv.
Elfstrand, P. (1946a), "Hamn, varv och sjöfart". In N. S. Norling, G. E. Lundén, & P. Humbla, *Ur Gävle stads historia*. Gävle.
Elfstrand, P. (1946b), "Ur förvaltningshistorien". In N. S. Norling, G. E. Lundén, & P. Humbla, *Ur Gävle stads historia*. Gävle.
Fyhrvall, O. (1904), *Gävle Stads sparbank 1824–1904, minnesskrift*. Stockholm.
Fyhrvall, O. (1913), *Gefleborgs Läns sparbank 1863–1913, minnesskrift*. Gefle.
Hellgren, H. (2003), *Fasta förbindelser*. Uppsala: Acta Universitatis Upsaliensis.
Hellner, B. (1946), "Skrå och hantverk". In N. S. Norling, G. E. Lundén, & P. Humbla, *Ur Gävle stads historia*. Gävle.
Historical statistics of Sweden Part 1. Population.
Gårdlund, T., Janelid, I., Ramström, D., & Lindblad, H. (1973), *Atlas Copco 1873–1973*.

Karlström, T. (1974), *Gävle Stadsbild. Bebyggelsehistoria och samhällsutveckling till 1900-talets början*. Gävle: Flanör bokhandel.

Larsson, M. (2010), "The State and the Financial System: Regulation and Regime Change Around 1900". In A. Ögren (ed.), *The Swedish Financial Revolution*. Basingstoke: Palgrave Macmillan.

Nygren, I. (1967), *Svensk sparbanksutlåning 1820–1913. En analys av större sparbankers kreditgivning*. Göteborg: Meddelanden från Ekonomisk-historiska institutionen vid Göteborgs universitet.

Sjölander, A. (2003), *Den naturliga ordning. Makt och intressen i de svenska sparbankerna 1882–1968*. Uppsala: Acta Universitatis Upsaliensis.

Sommarin, E. (1942), *Vårt sparbanksväsen 1834–1892*. Lund.

SOS, sparbanksstatistik 1895–1901 (Swedish savings banks statistics). Stockholm: Nordstedt & söner.

CHAPTER 7

Risk Management in Swedish Savings Banks—Concluding Remarks

Abstract This chapter concludes the book on risk management in early banking. The role of trust and legitimacy in the savings banks' lending and deposit markets are discussed. The risks connected with the relationship to customers are analyzed, with a special focus on the aspects of collaterals.

Keywords Theoretical feedback · Trust · Legitimacy · Risk management

Legitimacy and Trust—the Basis for Banking

In understanding the historical Swedish model for regulation of the financial markets, as well as other markets, it is important to recognize how the public authorities on the local, regional and national level were organized and how they were interconnected with each other. Sweden has since the sixteenth century been divided into about 20 counties, each governed by a county governor appointed by the king, later the parliament. The county governors were instrumental in the governing of the local and regional markets and they were obliged to annually report to the king/parliament on the general economic development in "their" county. The county governors were not only obliged to report on the specific development of the savings banks, as well as other banking institutions,

M. Larsson et al., *Risk Management in Early Banking*, Palgrave Studies in the History of Finance, https://doi.org/10.1007/978-3-030-80775-7_7

they were also strongly encouraged to contribute to the establishment of savings banks in every town and practically in every parish. In their ambition to fulfil this assignment, many of the county governors not only encouraged the establishment of savings banks, but they also stepped in as members of the boards in several savings banks. Hence, they could report on the development of the savings banks right from the inside.

This model for relocated state governing of banks and the regional financial markets proved to be both flexible and cost-efficient. Each county had its specific challenges on the banking and financial markets and by this model of "soft" regulation the state could at the same time have both sufficient insight into the market activities and the risk-taking of individual banks, and the possibility to intervene more directly whenever it was necessary. Despite some local and regional differences between savings banks, they were all regarded more as philanthropic than commercial institutions, albeit offering financial services in competition with other financial actors. This might also have helped to increase both legitimacy and public trust in savings banks.

The Swedish financial market underwent an extensive development in the 1820s and 1830s, which induced the modernization of the entire financial system. With the establishment of savings banks and commercial banks from the 1820s a new institutionalized structure was introduced, which gradually replaced financial actors such as business houses and private bankers. The establishment of savings and commercial banks also meant the birth of a stable savings market for those well-off but also for more impoverished people. However, these changes were not implemented promptly, it was rather a long-term process which lasted more or less the entire nineteenth century.

There was no tradition or experience connected with institutionalized savings markets in the early phases of the establishment of Swedish savings banks. Thus, there were no regulations protecting the depositors' capital, even though people previously had been able to deposit savings by private bankers or other local financial actors. For the savings banks it was of central importance to establish a general legitimacy to attract the potential customers—savers as well as borrowers. To create this confidence the savings banks utilized the good reputation of members of the local community. With these persons as principals and often as the initial depositors in the bank, a general legitimacy could be created, which attracted the capital from especially the less well-off in the community.

Legitimacy through legislation and the existence of confidence-inspiring people as founders were especially important in attracting new depositors to the savings banks. This is not surprising since savings were regarded as the basis for personal well-being in the long run and an important part of the savings banks philanthropic mission, which made the savings banks especially important for the development of the institutionally organized savings market. This was not a revolutionary development but rather an incremental long-term change. However, the lack of legislation for savings banks' capital administration and lending, made the personal trust between the bank and its borrowing customers and the use of self-regulation of larger importance—often influenced by the older credit system developed by trading houses and private bankers.

The savings banks' charters were especially important during the decades leading up to the regulation of 1875. A detailed and transparent company charter could replace an official legislation and create the necessary legitimacy. A company statute was also easier to adjust to changed economic conditions and was thus an important part of the self-regulation, which in some cases could help reduce risks. The implementation of a savings banks' law, on the other hand, created a standardization of savings banks' regulations and business and made official control of the savings banks' activities easier.

Seen over the nineteenth century; personal trust as well as legitimacy played important roles for the savings banks' development. Legitimacy created through official and semi-official regulation as well as the personal involvement of trustworthy persons as for example founders, were important for the attraction of savings. This situation did not change much during the nineteenth century, besides that the legislation for savings banks (1892) became more important than the charters. From the start, the relationship between the savings banks and their borrowers was based on personal trust and self-regulation since the legislation did not explicitly cope with this question. This contributed to some diversification between banks, especially in the selection of customers but also the use of collaterals—which will be shown in the latter part of this chapter.

Managing Credit Risks

Most Swedish savings banks devoted the majority of their investments to lending. This gave a higher rate of return than investments in bonds and shares. However, this policy fluctuated between years and savings banks. The years around 1870 were an important transitional period for the savings banks lending, when the traditional lending system characterized by networks, co-operation with other financial organizations and insider lending was gradually replaced by a system based on a larger and more heterogeneous number of borrowers. At the same time, it became increasingly difficult to have the same control of the borrowers as before, and this meant that credits with name collaterals gradually were replaced by mortgages. Thus, Swedish savings banks were often used for financing housing and community infrastructure especially in urban areas. In both Norway and Denmark savings banks held stronger market positions than in Sweden during the nineteenth century. This can to some extent be explained by these savings bank's active lending to the expanding companies in the local economies, while Swedish savings banks were subordinated to commercial banks (see Chapter 5).

Banks are affected by different financial risks of which several are interconnected. But for banks in the nineteenth century most of these risks were not relevant. Currency risks were of no importance for savings banks as both deposits and lending were handled in SEK. Interest rate risks on the other hand could be of importance for those banks that had a broad business including borrowing—short- as well as long term—from other actors on the financial market. However, this was not the case for savings banks, especially as business was built on deposits. A professional administration of deposits including investments in short-term securities, which could easily be transferred to cash, would also make it possible for savings banks to avoid liquidity crises.

The largest financial risk for savings banks in the nineteenth century was linked to credit management. It was necessary to evaluate both the risks connected to a potential borrower as well as the collaterals presented. From an overall perspective, mortgage collaterals were regarded as the most secure together with collaterals in financial securities. Name collaterals—which in the early development of the Swedish savings banks were the dominant form of collateral, were regarded as the riskiest. The use of name collaterals was an inheritance from the private non-institutional financiers—private bankers and trading houses—that preceded the establishment of savings and commercial banks.[1]

[1] Hellgren (2003) and Perlinge (2005).

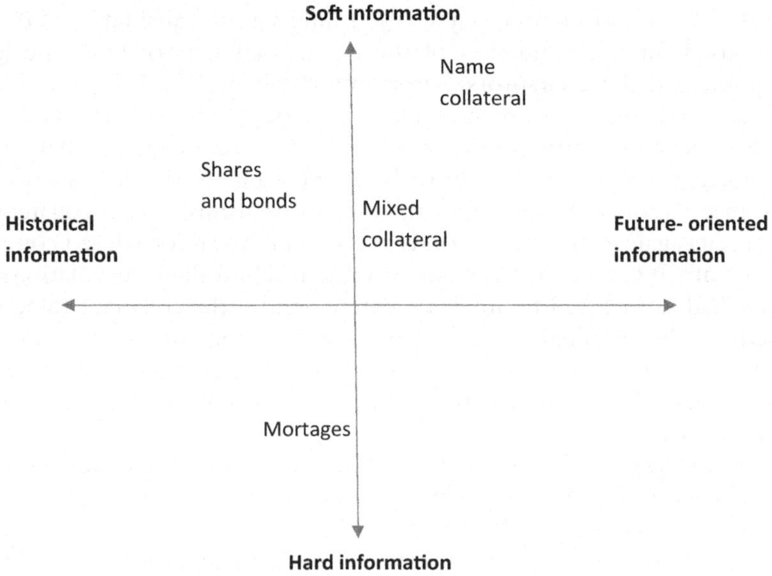

Fig. 7.1 Credit risk management in Swedish savings bank

It has been stated already that the use of different collaterals reflects savings banks' lending risks. The mortgages were primarily founded on the market value of the real estate, which was based on assessed value, or the fire insurance value. But the credit was only granted to a specific share of the estimated market value—in Gävle savings bank; 50 per cent of the fire insurance value (see Chapter 6). For larger investments in commercial properties and apartment buildings the calculated future annual returns were also of importance for the size on the mortgage. Thus, mortgages were foremost founded on hard information (calculations) based on market information, available from both historical information and calculations for the future (Fig. 7.1).[2]

Credits based on the mixture of mortgage and the good name of guarantors were used primarily as a mean to increase the value of loans for investments in construction and house reparations. These credits included

[2] The model used is inspired by Rad (2017).

not only hard information, but also soft information (qualitative information) used for the evaluation of the creditworthiness of both the loan applicant and the guarantors. These evaluations were primarily built on collected information from strategic informers, which made it possible to evaluate persons' future possibilities to fulfil their payments. As there were no mortgages involved in loans with name collaterals, the dependence on soft information was even larger than for loans against mixed collaterals.

Credits against shares and bonds as collaterals were considered comparatively safe in late twentieth century Sweden. Until then, speculations on shares had not existed to any large extent. And if the collateral value was based on the nominal value and not on the—sometimes fluctuating—market value the risks were considered low. The credit was then founded mostly on historical information and not on speculations on the future value of shares.

The managing of credit risks in Swedish savings banks was at least towards the end of the nineteenth century comparatively secure. The role of name collaterals had decreased, especially in value, while the use of mortgages and loans against shares and bonds had grown. This development resembles what happened in several other countries, but the decreased lending to for example companies made credit risks in Swedish savings banks possibly even lower. This became apparent in the 1910s and 1920s when commercial banks participated in speculations on the stock market and increased their lending to commercial activities, while saving banks bypassed these activities and thus managed to avoid the financial crisis in the early 1920s.

Most likely, this cautious attitude towards credits and credit risks can help explain why the savings banks' market share increased after 1920 and helped boost the savings banks legitimacy.

The dominating role of personal trust and social control in savings banks' lending in the early nineteenth century was gradually replaced by a general trust in the financial system and a public control. This happened towards the end of the nineteenth century, at the same time as legislation became more distinct, business increased and the competition from other financial actors grew. The financial system became more standardized based on legitimacy, instead of being dependent of personal assessments.

References

Hellgren, H. (2003), *Fasta förbindelser*. Uppsala: Acta Universitatis Upsaliensis.

Perlinge, A. (2005), *Sockenbankirerna. Kreditrelationer och tidig bankverksamhet. Vånga socken i Skåne 1840–1900*. Stockholm: Nordiska museets förlag.

Rad, A. (2017), *Bank Risk Management: How Do Bank Employees Deal with Risk at the Strategic and Operational Levels*. Sundsvall: Faculty of Human Society, Mid Sweden University.

Index

M. Larsson et al., *Risk Management in Early Banking*, Palgrave Studies in the History of Finance,
https://doi.org/10.1007/978-3-030-80775-7

The manufacturer's authorised representative in the EU is Springer Nature Customer Service Centre GmbH, Europaplatz 3, 69115 Heidelberg, Germany. If you have any concerns regarding our products, please contact ProductSafety@springernature.com

Printed and bound by CPI Group (UK) Ltd, Croydon, CR0 4YY
30/09/2026
02225466-0005